T0209452

An Analysis of

Pierre Bourdieu's

Outline of a Theory of Practice

Rodolfo Maggio

Published by Macat International Ltd
24:13 Coda Centre, 189 Munster Road, London SW6 6AW.

Distributed exclusively by Routledge
2 Park Square, Milton Park, Abingdon, Oxon OX14 4RN
711 Third Avenue, New York, NY 10017, USA

Routledge is an imprint of the Taylor & Francis Group, an informa business

www.macat.com
info@macat.com

Cataloguing in Publication Data
A catalogue record for this book is available from the British Library.
Library of Congress Cataloguing-in-Publication Data is available upon request.
Cover illustration: Jonathan Edwards

ISBN 978 1 912303 91 5 (hardback)
ISBN 978 1 912284 62 7 (paperback)
ISBN 978 1 912284 76 4 (e-book)

Notice
The information in this book is designed to orientate readers of the work under analysis,
to elucidate and contextualise its key ideas and themes, and to aid in the development
of critical thinking skills. It is not meant to be used, nor should it be used, as a
substitute for original thinking or in place of original writing or research. References and
notes are provided for informational purposes and their presence does not constitute
endorsement of the information or opinions therein. This book is presented solely for
educational purposes. It is sold on the understanding that the publisher is not engaged
to provide any scholarly advice. The publisher has made every effort to ensure that
this book is accurate and up-to-date, but makes no warranties or representations with
regard to the completeness or reliability of the information it contains. The information
and the opinions provided herein are not guaranteed or warranted to produce particular
results and may not be suitable for students of every ability. The publisher shall not be
liable for any loss, damage or disruption arising from any errors or omissions, or from
the use of this book, including, but not limited to, special, incidental, consequential or
other damages caused, or alleged to have been caused, directly or indirectly, by the
information contained within.

CONTENTS

THE MACAT LIBRARY

The Macat Library is a series of unique academic explorations of seminal works in the humanities and social sciences – books and papers that have had a significant and widely recognised impact on their disciplines. It has been created to serve as much more than just a summary of what lies between the covers of a great book. It illuminates and explores the influences on, ideas of, and impact of that book. Our goal is to offer a learning resource that encourages critical thinking and fosters a better, deeper understanding of important ideas.

Each publication is divided into three Sections: Influences, Ideas, and Impact. Each Section has four Modules. These explore every important facet of the work, and the responses to it.

This Section-Module structure makes a Macat Library book easy to use, but it has another important feature. Because each Macat book is written to the same format, it is possible (and encouraged!) to cross-reference multiple Macat books along the same lines of inquiry or research. This allows the reader to open up interesting interdisciplinary pathways.

To further aid your reading, lists of glossary terms and people mentioned are included at the end of this book (these are indicated by an asterisk [*] throughout) – as well as a list of works cited.

Macat has worked with the University of Cambridge to identify the elements of critical thinking and understand the ways in which six different skills combine to enable effective thinking.
Three allow us to fully understand a problem; three more give us the tools to solve it. Together, these six skills make up the **PACIER** model of critical thinking. They are:

ANALYSIS – understanding how an argument is built
EVALUATION – exploring the strengths and weaknesses of an argument
INTERPRETATION – understanding issues of meaning

CREATIVE THINKING – coming up with new ideas and fresh connections
PROBLEM-SOLVING – producing strong solutions
REASONING – creating strong arguments

To find out more, visit **WWW.MACAT.COM.**

CRITICAL THINKING AND *OUTLINE OF A THEORY OF PRACTICE*

Primary critical thinking skill: ANALYSIS
Secondary critical thinking skill: EVALUATION

Pierre Bourdieu's *Outline of a Theory of Practice* is a fundamental text in anthropology and sociology, and a superb tool for the reader to refine their analytical abilities. In order to write this book, Bourdieu, a sociologist himself, had to analyze a large quantity of material, ranging from ethnographic data collected during his experiences in Algeria, to the vast and complex literature produced by different schools of thought, to social phenomena in post-war French society. From him, the reader can learn how an argument is built, as well as how to deconstruct alternative and/or opposing arguments.

Bourdieu was able to break down the arguments advanced by structuralists on the one hand and phenomenologists and ethnomethodologists on the other regarding the best theory to understand why people act the way they do. In so doing, he classified the positions as being essentially opposed, which allowed him the theoretical clarity that was necessary to build his "third way."★ Bourdieu's evaluation of these different positions led him to consider the theoretical value of both, rather than simply dismissing them as unsuitable. Such a nuanced approach resulted in strengthening his theory against its critiques as well as broadening the applicability of his theory beyond its immediate field.

This widespread applicability, as well as the longevity of Bourdieu's theory of practice, proves that there is much to learn from his analytical methods and evaluative skills.

ABOUT THE AUTHOR OF THE ORIGINAL WORK

Pierre Bourdieu (1930–2002) was the most important sociologist of the last quarter of the twentieth century. His crucial contribution to the social sciences was first systematized in *Outline of a Theory of Practice*. He initially studied philosophy,* but then turned to anthropology after conducting ethnographic research in Kabylia during his military service in Algeria. The data he collected became the basis of a lifetime career of achievements, which have been recognized, both in France and beyond, with prestigious positions and awards.

ABOUT THE AUTHOR OF THE ANALYSIS

Dr. Rodolfo Maggio is an anthropologist currently working as a post-doctoral researcher at the University of Oxford. He holds a PhD in Social Anthropology from the University of Manchester and an MSc in Anthropology and Development from the London School of Economics and Political Science. As of today, he has written four Macat analyses.

ABOUT MACAT

GREAT WORKS FOR CRITICAL THINKING

Macat is focused on making the ideas of the world's great thinkers accessible and comprehensible to everybody, everywhere, in ways that promote the development of enhanced critical thinking skills.

It works with leading academics from the world's top universities to produce new analyses that focus on the ideas and the impact of the most influential works ever written across a wide variety of academic disciplines. Each of the works that sit at the heart of its growing library is an enduring example of great thinking. But by setting them in context – and looking at the influences that shaped their authors, as well as the responses they provoked – Macat encourages readers to look at these classics and game-changers with fresh eyes. Readers learn to think, engage and challenge their ideas, rather than simply accepting them.

'Macat offers an amazing first-of-its-kind tool for interdisciplinary learning and research. Its focus on works that transformed their disciplines and its rigorous approach, drawing on the world's leading experts and educational institutions, opens up a world-class education to anyone.'

Andreas Schleicher
Director for Education and Skills, Organisation for Economic Co-operation and Development

'Macat is taking on some of the major challenges in university education ... They have drawn together a strong team of active academics who are producing teaching materials that are novel in the breadth of their approach.'

Prof Lord Broers,
former Vice-Chancellor of the University of Cambridge

'The Macat vision is exceptionally exciting. It focuses upon new modes of learning which analyse and explain seminal texts which have profoundly influenced world thinking and so social and economic development. It promotes the kind of critical thinking which is essential for any society and economy.
This is the learning of the future.'

Rt Hon Charles Clarke, former UK Secretary of State for Education

'The Macat analyses provide immediate access to the critical conversation surrounding the books that have shaped their respective discipline, which will make them an invaluable resource to all of those, students and teachers, working in the field.'

Professor William Tronzo, University of California at San Diego

WAYS IN TO THE TEXT

KEY POINTS

- Pierre Bourdieu was a French philosopher, anthropologist, and sociologist widely known for his theory of practice.

- *Outline of a Theory of Practice* is Bourdieu's first attempt to theorize human action systematically.

- Bourdieu's theory of practice has been influential in the social sciences.

Who Was Pierre Bourdieu?

Pierre Bourdieu was born in the French small village of Denguin in 1930. His father was a farmer who later became a postman in the village of Lasseube, in south-western France. His mother was of a similar social origin, although her family owned some land in Lasseube. At home, his parents spoke Gascon—the regional language.

Bourdieu studied in a local school and attended the main Lycée* in Pau. Subsequently, he gained admission to the prestigious Lycée Louis-le-Grand* in Paris, where he completed his secondary education. This led to him entering the École Normale Supérieure* in 1951, where he studied philosophy under the tutelage of the famous Marxist* scholar Louis Althusser* and graduated as a laureate (*agrégé*) in 1955. Jacques Derrida* was also a fellow at that time, and Jean-Paul Sartre* had studied there previously.

Bourdieu's academic career took a significant turn when, dissatisfied with the education system, he refused to write the thesis required for his graduation. In addition, in 1955 he was conscripted* to fight in the Algerian War of Independence.* Both of these events deeply influenced his intellectual productions.

First, the rejection of the elitist education system in France led him to explore the cultural reproductive mechanisms of the social classes. Second, the ethnographic* study he conducted in Kabylia,* a region of northern Algeria, inspired some of the ideas and concepts he later developed in *Outline*, first published in 1972.

A third major influence was the academic environment of the time. The structuralists* argued that structures,* such as rules, norms, and patterns of thought, are the ultimate determinants of people's actions. In contrast, phenomenology* and ethnomethodology* explained individual behaviors in terms of human agency,* the ability to act with a certain degree of individual freedom. Bourdieu rejected both of these approaches. In *Outline*, he sought to explain human action in a different way.

What Does *Outline* Say?

Outline addresses one of the central questions of sociology:* what determines human actions?

In addressing this question Bourdieu rejected structuralism, the idea that the ultimate determinants of human behavior are innate structures in the human mind. He rejected also phenomenology and ethnomethodology, two approaches that insisted on the primacy of individual experiences to account for human action, as opposed to pre-existing structures.

Hence, in order to understand Bourdieu's theory, one must grasp the following concepts. First, structure is the universal human tendency to classify experience in terms of binary* oppositions, such as male/female, raw/cooked, pure/impure, and to act on their basis.

Second, the concept of agency refers to the ability of social actors to act independently of structures and rules. In order to mediate between structure and agency, Bourdieu introduced the concept of "habitus,"* the attitudes that actors internalize while being conditioned by past experiences, and re-enact in present everyday practices, though with a certain degree of freedom.

Actors manifest their course of action in a "field,"* a fourth major concept indicating the space where they compete for power and influence using their "symbolic capital,"* which includes social capital* (such as the networks and contacts available to the actors) and cultural capital* (like the books they read and the knowledge they have). Bourdieu introduced these concepts to show that economic capital* is not the only resource actors possess to compete in a field, impose a vision on others, and reproduce unequal power relations.

Thus, with *Outline* Bourdieu moved beyond abstract categories, such as structure and agency, which he considered means for putting oneself in a superior, objectifying* position. By assuming such a stance, social scientists* are unable to see that social action is fundamentally relational. Rather than engaging in distant observations, Bourdieu believed that social scientists should produce accounts that are embedded in context.

Bourdieu also noted that, like all actors, social scientists are always part of the practice that they observe. As a consequence, they influence it with their observation and therefore cannot be unbiased. This is an example of how the definition of social phenomena,* rather than being either objective or subjective, depends on interactions.

With *Outline* Bourdieu became a dominant scholar in French sociology. Later, his translated works inspired and challenged scholars in other countries. For example, the engaging approach of *Outline* challenged American quantitative sociologists* because measurements require detachment from the context, and even then, it is not clear how symbolic capital can be measured. The text was also very influential among British sociologists. As a consequence of this widespread influence, Bourdieu transformed sociology and anthropology,* as well as other disciplines.

Indeed, after Bourdieu it has become increasingly difficult for scholars in these fields to take either the objectivist or the subjectivist approach. However, a number of serious criticisms have also been formulated against Bourdieu's theory of practice. It follows that in order to understand the meaning and significance of *Outline*, it is necessary to examine it detail.

Why Does *Outline* Matter?

Outline is Bourdieu's first attempt to systematize his theory of practice. Therefore, anyone interested in understanding Bourdieu's work overall should become familiar with the text.

The theory of practice is a set of concepts, including habitus, field, and symbolic capital, with which Bourdieu challenged both the methods and epistemology* of the social sciences. However, Bourdieu has not simply contributed to a debate, but rather, he has transformed the terms of the debate.[1]

Still, as the title of the book suggests, the text provides only an *outline*. It is not a fully accomplished account of the practice theory, but rather a first attempt to systematically formulate a concept that Bourdieu continued to refine for over three decades. Nevertheless, the main pillars of the theory are there, which is why the impact of the text has been so widespread.

In 1996, *Contemporary Sociology*[2] recognized *Outline* as one of the ten most influential contributions to the field of the previous 25 years. In addition, *Outline* has had a considerable influence on many other disciplines, including anthropology, social psychology,* organizational sociology,* cultural analysis,* management,* and many others. Therefore, *Outline* is essential reading for anyone who seeks to understand the development of the social sciences in the second half of the twentieth century, and particularly the vocabulary that is currently used to analyze and describe social phenomena.

At the time of his early writings, Bourdieu saw that the sociology and anthropology of the 1940s and 50s were unable to explain human action. The reason for this, he argued, was that these disciplines were blind to the drawbacks of structuralism and phenomenology. The former approach placed excessive emphasis on the repressive power of pre-existing social structures, and the latter insisted too much on the unbound freedom of the individual actor.

Understanding how Bourdieu tried to correct these approaches provides a concrete example of how different sociological currents interact and how the outcomes of such interaction made the social sciences what they are today. In conclusion, in addition to understanding the content of Bourdieu's *Outline* it is essential to appreciate the intellectual environment that influenced it, as well as the impact it had on the social sciences and beyond.

NOTES

1   Michèle Lamont, "How has Bourdieu been good to think with? The case of the United States." *Sociological Forum*. 27.1, Blackwell Publishing (2012): 228.

2   Craig Calhoun, "A Different Poststructuralism," *Contemporary Sociology* 25.3 (1996): 302–305.

SECTION 1
INFLUENCES

THE AUTHOR AND THE HISTORICAL CONTEXT

KEY POINTS

- *Outline of a Theory of Practice* is the first systematization of Bourdieu's thinking.

- Bourdieu's experience as an ethnographer in Algeria deeply influenced his work.

- The education system and changes in post-war France also inspired Bourdieu's scholarship.

Why Read This Text?

Pierre Bourdieu is widely regarded as the greatest sociologist of the last quarter of the twentieth century.[1] *Outline of a Theory of Practice* holds a very important place in the author's corpus. It contains his first attempt to systematize his thinking in order to make it applicable to other problems and disciplines. Bourdieu's work continues to be influential in sociology, anthropology, education, and other disciplines in the social sciences.

While no social scientist denies the importance of Bourdieu's work, its usage is in dispute. For example, Anthony King* argued that the concept of habitus did not resolve the opposition between subjectivity* and objectivity* in social sciences. Still, King admits that "despite the failings of the habitus," Bourdieu "offers a way out of the structure–agency problem without relapsing into either subjectivism* or objectivism."[*2]

So, notwithstanding the critiques, scholars such as those in the Bourdieu Study Group* defend parts of Bourdieu's work and its application to the social sciences. They recognize that there might be

> **❝** I have never accepted the separation between the theoretical construction of the object of research and the set of practical procedures without which there can be no real knowledge. I have combated untheoretical empiricism* vigorously enough to be also able to reject the unempirical conceptualization of the pure 'theorician'. **❞**
>
> Pierre Bourdieu, *The Struggle for Symbolic Order*

problems with his theory, such as what they see as the absence of individual choice in the concept of habitus.[3] Still, for them, thinking *with* Bourdieu is more fruitful and rewarding than dismissing it. For these thinkers, the challenge is to develop an awareness of misusing Bourdieu and creatively adapt his methods and approaches. Hence, while some parts of Bourdieu's framework have been criticized, others have been favored and are still being applied.

It follows that the complete and "mechanical imitation" of Bourdieu's approach is considered uncritical.[4] Indeed, his theoretical depth and engagement with other theories and methodologies touches the core of the social sciences. Thus, anyone who is interested in the objectives and methods of social inquiry and the mechanisms of societies and cultures must become familiar with his work.

Author's Life

Bourdieu's personal experiences influenced his academic work. However, the way in which this influence should be interpreted has been contested. "According to his most faithful English translator, Richard Nice, there is a myth—'the peasant boy confronting urban civilisation'—and there is a more serious version of Bourdieu's life, that of a 'petit bourgeois* and a success story'."[5]

The myth relates to Bourdieu's humble origins. Coming from a modest family background, he had to work harder than his more privileged peers to be admitted into distinguished French schools. Consequently, he was critical of the elitism* of the French education system. In fact, one of his most significant works dealt with the inequalities of French society, where social origins rather than individual competencies determined the educational success of individuals.

While the narrative of the humble origins might be overemphasized, there is no doubt that Bourdieu worked hard to achieve his position. Upon returning from Algeria in 1960, he worked as a research assistant at the Faculty of Arts of the University of Paris. After only three years he became Director of Studies at the *École pratique des hautes études,** he created the *Centre de Sociologie Européenne** in 1968, and in 1981 he became chair at the prestigious *Collège de France.** He received the *Médaille d'or* du *Centre National de la Recherche Scientifique,** the Goffman Prize* from the University of California, Berkeley, and the Huxley Medal* of the Royal Anthropological Institute. These achievements would have been extraordinary even for a *petit bourgeois.*

So, while Bourdieu's career trajectory might not have begun in the fields, as retold in the story of the peasant boy, it is not possible to underestimate his hard work and the resulting achievements in both French academia and international scholarship.

Author's Background

The political and socio-economic context of mid-twentieth century France profoundly influenced Bourdieu's intellectual productions.

Reflecting upon the inequalities in the education system, Bourdieu realized that educational success could not be explained as a result of the economic capital of families or of individuals. He preferred instead to explain differences in educational performances as the result of *cultural* capital. Cultural capital does not include material goods. Rather, it belongs to those people who have access to, and understand the meanings of, *cultural* goods (museums, philosophical debates, movies, etc.), which they can translate into educational success and social mobility. This conceptualization of cultural capital became one of the most widely adopted concepts in Bourdieu's work.

Another historical aspect that deeply influenced his thinking was his conscription into military service for the colonial war against Algeria. In France at the time, the process of modernization, the collapse of the Fourth Republic,* the rise in prices, population growth, and civil unrest resulted in tensions between different social, political, and ethnic groups.[6] Bourdieu was fascinated by these tensions. In Algeria, he also witnessed tensions, in this case those of a traditional society facing the imposed values of a colonizing power. These observations in France and in Algeria, along with his experiences of education, resulted in his focus on social inequality and his move away from philosophy towards sociology, and subsequently anthropology.

Indeed, his ethnographic fieldwork among the Berbers of Kabylia turned him into an anthropologist, albeit a self-taught one. Upon his return to France, he began attending Claude Lévi-Strauss's* seminars at the *Collège de France and his ethnology** lectures at the *Musée de l'Homme.*

This diversity of contexts in which Bourdieu developed as a scholar might partly explain why his work has been so influential in a diversity of disciplines.

NOTES

1   Elizabeth Silva and Alan Warde, "Introduction: the importance of Bourdieu," in *Cultural analysis and Bourdieu's legacy: settling accounts and developing alternatives*, ed. Elizabeth Silva and Alan Warde (London: Routledge, 2010), 1.

2   Anthony King, "Thinking with Bourdieu against Bourdieu: A 'practical' critique of the habitus." *Sociological Theory 18.3 (2000): 417*–433.

3   Jessie Abrahams, Nicola Ingram, Jenny Thatcher, and Ciaran Burke, *Bourdieu: The Next Generation: The Development of Bourdieu's Intellectual Heritage in Contemporary UK Sociology* (London: Routledge), 2.

4   Nicolas Truong and Nicolas Weill, "A decade after his death, French sociologist Pierre Bourdieu stands tall," *Guardian* 2012. Accessed July 19, 2017. https://www.theguardian.com/world/2012/feb/21/pierre-bourdieu-philosophy-most-quoted.

5   Richard Jenkins, *Pierre Bourdieu* (London: Routledge, 2014), 3.

6   P. N. Rastogi, "The course of French society (1955–73) – a simulation." *Simulation 22 (1974): 119–123.*

MODULE 2
ACADEMIC CONTEXT

KEY POINTS

- *Outline of a Theory of Practice* seeks to explain the principles at the basis of human action.

- Structuralists, existentialists, post-modernists,* and quantitative sociologists had different views of what constitutes human action.

- Bourdieu was influenced by the realist* tradition in the social sciences.

The Work In Its Context

In order to understand Pierre Bourdieu's concerns for the legacy of the social sciences it is important for readers to comprehend the historical context at the time he wrote the book. Bourdieu allocated the first chapter to the problems that he saw in the intellectual battlefield of the time.

Broadly speaking, four streams of research were dominant at the time Bourdieu authored his text. Structuralists had proposed that structures were the ultimate regulators of human actions, and that societies maintain their stability through the endurance of these structures.

The residents of the rival camp, broadly speaking, were the existentialists who favored the agent's freedom of choice in determining their actions. This group of intellectuals included phenomenologists and ethnomethodologists, who emphasized the perspective of the agent rather than the structure, and explained human action as agency.

> **❝** I feel that many characteristics shared by the 'structuralist' generation of Althusser, Foucault,* etc. ... derive from their effort to distinguish themselves from existentialism* and all that it entailed in their eyes: that insipid 'humanism' that was prevalent, the preference for 'lived experience' and that form of political moralism ...**❞**
>
> Pierre Bourdieu, *The Struggle for Symbolic Order*

Bourdieu disagreed with both. He thought neither structure nor agency were adequate explanations of social action. Being discontent with both views, in *Outline* Bourdieu endeavors to provide an account of human action that transcends them.

In addition, Bourdieu is critical of the rejection of rationality and synthetic theories, typical of post-modern thinking. He found this attitude dangerous because, he claimed, it destroyed concepts developed in the history of sociology, like society, state, and community. He thought these wre important constituents of our understanding, which should not be dismissed, but rather understood with a new theory, a theory of practice.

Finally, he considered quantitative methods as complementary to studies of human action, rather than fundamental. While they are unable to explain human actions on their own, they can be used along with qualitative methods.

Overview Of The Field

Among the various intellectual traditions that were popular in France at the time of Bourdieu's work, four are particularly noteworthy.

First, there was structuralism. The meaning of structure originates in the work of the Swiss linguist Ferdinand de Saussure.* Saussure distinguished between two parts of language: *parole* (the visible, subjective practice of speech) and *langue* (the underlying, objective structure of grammar rules). Following this method of binary opposition* between practice and structure, Lévi-Strauss posited that a combination of implicit and explicit rules—the structure—govern human actions. Thus, according to structural anthropology,* human actions are not free, but regulated.

Second, there was what Bourdieu called phenomenology and ethnomethodology,[1] which were influenced by existentialism, a very popular philosophical view at the time, mainly championed by Jean-Paul Sartre. Existentialism prioritizes human choice and subjectivity over and above every other aspect of the social world. This view influenced the phenomenological approach, particularly relevant in the work of Maurice Merleau-Ponty* and Martin Heidegger.* It also influenced ethnomethodology, which represented social actors as free to choose how to construct their reality and, thus, whether to respect the rules or not.

Third, a post-modern turn had occurred in the contemporary philosophy championed by Derrida and Foucault. For them, linguistic formations and discourses, rather than structures or agencies, were the key to understanding human actions.

The fourth stream was made up of those scholars in American sociology who placed most emphasis on statistical methods and Rational Choice Theory (RCT).* RCT viewed opportunistic behavior as the main determinant of individual decisions. While individuals are free to choose, the range of actions they take is restricted by their orientation towards the most rational option, namely profit maximization.

Academic Influences

Bourdieu challenged many authors and intellectual traditions. However, he borrowed simultaneously concepts and methods from other authors, often reinterpreting and appropriating them. It follows that the totality of his academic influences is rather complex and thus difficult to systematize.

In a broader sense, Bourdieu belongs to the realist tradition in the social sciences. Realism "starts off from the position that things social are rarely, if ever, as they seem. Their reality or essence must be discovered beneath the surface world of what people do and say in social interaction."[2] One such example is the relations of production,* where the worker's product is alienated* rather than appropriated as the result of their work.

Regarding realist thinkers, Bourdieu draws particularly on the works of Karl Marx.* In his own work, Marx had built on Georg W.F. Hegel's* dialectic* to conceptualize the development that *underlies* human history. However, instead of following the idealist* approach of the Hegelian school,* which stressed the importance of ideas, Marx took a materialist* approach, termed historical materialism,* which focused more on human relations. What Marx did with Hegel, Bourdieu did with the structural method of Lévi-Strauss, which he found overtly abstract, and attempted to ground it in the material relations between social actors.[3] For example, while Lévi-Strauss analyzed marriage prescriptions as indicators of underlying structures to explain human actions, Bourdieu looked at whether the Kabyle people (Berbers inhabiting northern Algeria) actually followed those marital rules or not, and the meaning they attached to them.

Then, the concept of a reproducing mechanism was perhaps borrowed from the functionalist* theories of Émile Durkheim.* Bourdieu was also influenced by the concept, of domination as the product of ideology and legitimizing discourses developed by Max Weber.* For Bourdieu, however, domination is not conscious, for people who are dominated cannot fully realize their condition.[4]

Thus, rather than mere inspiration, Bourdieu's attitude is to adopt the views of these thinkers critically. He calls this critical attitude *Marx against Marx*, *Durkheim against Durkheim*, and *Weber against Weber*.[5]

NOTES

1   Pierre Bourdieu, *Outline of a Theory of Practice* (Cambridge: Cambridge University Press, 1977), 3.

2   Richard Jenkins, *Pierre Bourdieu* (London: Routledge, 2014), 16.

3   Jenkins, *Pierre Bourdieu*, 20.

4   Hans Joas and Wolfgang Knöbl, "Between Structuralism and Theory of Practice: The Cultural Sociology of Pierre Bourdieu," in *The Legacy of Pierre Bourdieu: Critical Essays*, ed. Simon Susen and Bryan Turner (London: Anthem Press, 2011), 25.

5   Michael Grenfell, *Pierre Bourdieu: Agent Provocateur* (London: Continuum, 2004), 200.

MODULE 3
THE PROBLEM

KEY POINTS

- *Outline of a Theory of Practice* addresses the question: what is human action and how can it be understood?

- Structuralists and existentialists saw structure and agency respectively as the ultimate determinants of human actions.

- Bourdieu partly rejected existent theories of action and partly drew upon them to develop his own.

Core Question

Pierre Bourdieu clearly expressed his challenge in the following sentence: "all of my thinking started from this point: how can behaviour be regulated without being the product of obedience to rules?"[1] Although his intellectual trajectory was influenced by the idea of structure as a set of rules that govern human actions, Bourdieu was never persuaded that human actions are only a means to realize abstract norms. If structure is inadequate for explaining human action—as Bourdieu argues throughout the book—then the question is, what governs human actions?

Consequently, one of the main aims of *Outline of a Theory of Practice* is to critically evaluate the theoretical approaches to human action that were previously developed in sociology and anthropology. Having identified the weaknesses in those approaches, Bourdieu's second main aim was to develop an alternative framework for understanding human action in the social world.

In order to achieve the first aim, the book discusses the epistemological and methodological premises of the social sciences

> ❝ In accepting as obligatory alternatives the model and the situation, the structure and the individual variations, one condemns oneself simply to take the diametrically opposite course to the structuralist abstraction which subsumes variations—regarded as simple variants—into the structure. ❞
>
> Bourdieu, *Outline of a Theory of Practice*

and argues that the earlier thinkers had failed to explain human action. Structuralists fail to explain human action because they see actors as obeying rules, without taking into consideration the diversity of choices that individuals can actually enact. Individuals, for them, can only reproduce the pre-existing structures that can be identified in their language and their thought. In contrast, existentialists, or (as Bourdieu calls them) phenomenologists and ethnomethodologists, cannot see the patterns in human actions because they only concentrate on individual instances of human action.

These approaches thus have neither predictive nor descriptive power. Following from that, Bourdieu seeks to address the inadequacy of these approaches in exploring and explaining social phenomena as they occur in the real world. In order to achieve this second aim, Bourdieu examines the *practice* instead of the *theory* of action. The concept that Bourdieu develops as a result of this examination is habitus.

The Participants

When Bourdieu started working on *Outline*, the participants in the debate about human action were, generally speaking, existentialists and structuralists.

A dominant figure in French existentialism was the philosopher Jean-Paul Sartre. His thinking was influenced by German philosophers like Martin Heidegger and Edmund Husserl.* However, it is important to note that Heidegger wrote a set of letters implying that Sartre misunderstood his book *Being and Time* while developing his own vision of human existence. Sartre's existentialism emphasized the freedom of choice and dominance that actors possess over structures, whereas Heidegger did not think that being necessarily precedes action. In any case, Sartre's existentialism, with its focus on individuality and liberty, offered an emancipatory view of life that was potentially appealing during World War II when life and death were daily matters.[2] Existentialism influenced what Bourdieu called phenomenological and ethnomethodological approaches to knowledge, namely the tendency to explain phenomena in terms of agency, which he regarded as shallow and a-theoretical.

The structuralism of Lévi-Strauss stood in opposition to these approaches. He conducted a series of ethnographic studies, as did Bourdieu, but his conclusions were markedly different. He argued that human action is essentially a reproduction of one's culture that is governed by structural rules. It is not a result of one's choices, but largely beyond one's control and even consciousness. Structures, indeed, are rooted in thought and language, as suggested by the Swiss structural linguist Saussure and by his American counterpart, Roman Jakobson.* Bourdieu was conscious of the criticisms advanced against structuralist theories of human action: (1) while practices change through time, structuralism does not account for change; (2) structuralists are not interested in how structure is played out in real life; and (3) they may just be imagining structures where there might well be nothing but practice.

The Contemporary Debate

The relationship between *Outline* and its immediate intellectual environment is twofold. On the one hand, it is critical to the priority that many of Bourdieu's contemporaries gave to theory over practice.

In this respect, he once said, "I can state without exaggeration that I resisted with all my strength the trendy forms of structuralism—which seem at times to be the only ones that were received abroad—when I tried to introduce structural, or relational, ideas into sociology. I also found the mechanistic application of Saussure and Jakobson unacceptable."[3]

On the other hand, Bourdieu wrote *Outline* in conversation with other schools of thought in social sciences. Hence, the book must be understood as based on Bourdieu's attitude towards the other dominant theories of human action and his lifetime commitment to propose an alternative theory.

In particular, the book questions the objectivism implied by structural anthropologists like Lévi-Strauss. Bourdieu contends that it is inaccurate to privilege "the structure of signs [or rules] ... at the expense of their practical functions."[4] While structuralists view social rules as the ultimate director of human action, Bourdieu argues that codified rules do not govern actions. It is the habitus, the "orchestrated improvisation of common dispositions"[5] that does it. Therefore, the text builds upon received ideas in contemporary literature, such as structure and agency, but rethinks them in innovative ways.

It follows that, in a sense, it was only possible to conceive of practice theory because structuralism, as well as other theories, was already there. Bourdieu challenged and modified the ideas of his contemporaries rather than dismissing or accepting them. He synthesized them and came up with a third way that was more than a mere continuation of, or opposition to them.

NOTES

1   Pierre Bourdieu, *In Other Words: Essays Toward a Reflexive Sociology* (Stanford University Press, 1990), 65.

2   Michael Grenfell, *Pierre Bourdieu: Key Concepts* (Durham: Acumen, 2008), 22.

3   Pierre Bourdieu, "The struggle for symbolic order." *Theory, Culture and Society* 3.3 (1986): 38.

4   Pierre Bourdieu, *Outline of a Theory of Practice* (Cambridge: Cambridge University Press, 1977), 24.

5   Bourdieu, *Outline*, 17.

THE AUTHOR'S CONTRIBUTION

KEY POINTS

- Bourdieu's aim was to explain what governs human action and illustrate his sociological method without producing abstract ideas.

- Bourdieu's approach was to transcend the structure/agency opposition with less rigid conceptualizations than previous authors.

- Bourdieu borrowed the concept of habitus from previous authors and appropriated it to the structure/agency debate.

Author's Aims

In composing *Outline of a Theory of Practice* Pierre Bourdieu had two distinct and interrelated aims. At a thematic level, he focuses on the question, what governs human action? At an epistemological level, he asks how social scientists can answer this question.

Although Bourdieu focuses on the question of human action, his aim is not necessarily to answer it in a straightforward way. He was influenced by previous and contemporary thinkers, but he did not develop a theory of social action in the same way as they did. Although *Outline* builds upon an attempt to transcend the classical dualisms prevalent in social theory (subjectivism/objectivism, structure/agency, micro/macro, etc.) the theory it offers is a "theory of practice," which Bourdieu did not consider as a theory in its conventional form. His book should not be read as an attempt to generate another theoretical body of ideas, but as a theory as embodied in practice.

> **❝** Of all the oppositions that artificially divide social science, the most fundamental … is the one that is set up between subjectivism and objectivism. … To move beyond the antagonism between these two modes of knowledge, … it is necessary to make explicit the presuppositions that they have in common as theoretical modes of knowledge. **❞**
>
> Pierre Bourdieu, *The Logic of Practice*

Bourdieu has achieved his aim to the extent that *Outline* is indeed a theory embodied in practice. However, as such, it is a very difficult theory to understand, precisely because it resists the tendency to adopt theoretical reasoning to produce abstract ideas. Rather than abstract ideas, Bourdieu aimed to produce a theory of practice, as the title of the book reads. For him, since practice is inherently complex, so should be the theory that aims to describe it.

As for the epistemological and methodological aspect of the text, Bourdieu attempted to avoid the extreme consequences of structuralism and subjectivism. "This is to be achieved, he suggests, by means of an epistemological break, not only with … reality, but also with the research process which produces an account of that reality."[1] To the extent that Bourdieu has profoundly influenced the epistemology of social sciences, he has achieved this second aim.

Approach

Bourdieu's approach is original in two broad senses. On the one hand, it opposes the dualities suggested by structuralism and existentialism that were prevalent at the time. On the other, it energizes a new account for social action on the basis of pre-existing approaches. Both contributions resulted from Bourdieu's experience as a self-taught ethnographer in Algeria first, and as an academic in France later.

In Algeria, he conducted his fieldwork among the Kabyle Berbers and became dissatisfied with the social theories of action of the time. These theories could not explain his observations of Kabyle rites, myths, and practices. Therefore, he strove to reconsider them in light of his findings and formulate a new theoretical framework for social action.

Bourdieu's approach opposed both structuralism and existentialism, for he saw them as unable to understand what human action really is. However, his work can also be seen as direct continuation of earlier works by other grand theorists in anthropology and sociology, in particular sociologists like Karl Marx, Max Weber, and Émile Durkheim.

More specifically, Marx inspired Bourdieu's understanding of society as the embodiment of concrete relationships rather than separate, abstract entities, like individuals and rules. Weber had formulated concepts such as domination, which Bourdieu developed as unconscious internalization of relations of subjugation. Ernst Cassirer* wrote about violence, power, and capital as "symbolic forms," which is very similar to the symbolic capital conceptualized by Bourdieu. From Durkheim, as much as from structural linguistics, Bourdieu borrowed the notion of structure and its reproducing mechanisms. However, he conceptualized it in an innovative, less rigid way by means of the concept of habitus.

Contribution In Context

The ideas in *Outline* are original to Bourdieu. However, he often utilizes terms and concepts in his theory that were previously used by other thinkers. In so doing, he appropriates these terms with the specific meaning that he ascribes to them. That is in strong opposition to the post-modernist tendency, prevalent at time, to deconstruct the concepts of the scientific discourse inscribed in the legacy of science, disempowering them as a consequence. Such was the approach taken by contemporaries like Derrida and Foucault.

Bourdieu, instead, compares and contrasts his work with that of other theorists. For instance, he borrowed the notion of *doxa** from Husserl and the concept of capital from Marx. However, the framework that he builds and the theory of practice that he suggests are new to both philosophy and sociology.

As for the concept of habitus, it can be traced back to Aristotle's* notion of *hexis*, which the Greek philosopher used to indicate the possession of a habit or disposition. However, in its contemporary usage, habitus was introduced into social theory by Marcel Mauss*[2] who saw it as a set of learned habits, including body attitudes, skills, and intuitions. It also closely resonates with Husserl's *Habitualität* and Hegel's *ethos*. All these authors had used a form of habitus to refer to a set of habitual dispositions,* which guide actors in their social life.

Bourdieu's usage, however, is different from the past usages. Habitus conveys not only the singular instances of social action, but also the very history that each individual carries, which structures his or her behavior. It is not the mere product of structures, for it depends also on practices and strategies.

NOTES

1   Richard Jenkins, *Pierre Bourdieu*. (London: Routledge, 2014), 11.

2   Pierre Bourdieu and Loïc J. D. Wacquant, (eds.) *An Invitation to Reflexive Sociology* (Cambridge: Cambridge Polity Press, 1992), 121.

SECTION 2
IDEAS

MAIN IDEAS

KEY POINTS

- The key themes of *Outline of a Theory of Practice* are: structure, agency, habitus, and the epistemology of the social sciences.

- Bourdieu argues that social scientists should understand human action as emerging from habitus rather than structure or agency.

- In his theory, Bourdieu uses complex language to represent the complexity of practice.

Key Themes

Outline of a Theory of Practice consists of four chapters that together form the basis of Pierre Bourdieu's contribution.

In the first chapter, "The Objective Limits of Objectivism," Bourdieu examines and evaluates previous social studies that explained human action as governed by explicit formal rules. By objectivism, Bourdieu refers to those attempts in social sciences that try to explain social phenomena as sustained by a set of structures. In this chapter, Bourdieu develops a critique towards this view, rejecting the idea that structures govern human actions.

The most significant chapter of the book is the second, "Structures and the Habitus." Here Bourdieu answers the question posed in the preceding chapter: if human action is not determined by the structures of explicit rules, then how can human action be theorized? Bourdieu's answer is that social action can be explained as resulting from the habitus. Habitus is "a system of lasting and transposable dispositions which, integrating past experiences, functions at every moment as a

> ❝ It is this attempt to thread a dialectical middle way or third path between the thesis and antithesis of objectivism and subjectivism which distinguishes Bourdieu's project. By objectifying the position of the social scientist as a competent actor in his/her own social world(s), as well as the position of the research subjects, ... and thus was the epistemological break made. ❞
>
> Richard Jenkins, *Pierre Bourdieu*

matrix of perceptions, appreciations and actions and makes possible the achievement of infinitely diversified tasks."[1]

The introduction of this concept allows Bourdieu to link structures—a priori, a set of rules, norms, and values in the context of social action—to the practices of actors. Simultaneously, habitus reflects the subjective dimension in Bourdieu's work without romanticizing actors as limitless free agents. In this way, Bourdieu founded his new approach to human action through the conceptualization of habitus as a bridge between structure and agency.

Exploring The Ideas

Outline starts with a critique of objectivism, the tendency to understand phenomena as readily understandable as if they were objects that scientists could observe unbiasedly. Bourdieu criticizes this attitude in the field of social sciences and its application to the study of social action. Objectivism in social research leads to understanding social life as resulting essentially from the application of rules.

In opposition to this view of social life, Bourdieu presents evidence from his ethnography among the Berber peasantry of Algeria. He argues that the practices he observed do not take the form of codified rules. Rules are memorable, explicit, and transferable, whereas the basic interactions between the people are implicit, specific, and depend on improvisation and temporary strategies. Hence, rules and practices should be distinguished.

For example, even though the Kabyle people assert that the marriage between patrilateral parallel cousins* is the preferred marriage rule, in practice only a tiny percentage of the Kabyle population marry according to it. This suggests that such kinds of explicit rules do not explain nor predict what actually happens, which is how they were understood from the objectivist perspectives in social sciences. Therefore, Bourdieu proposes that social practices are not accessible through universal a priori rules. Rather, they are fuzzy and their logic is opaque.

Building upon this conclusion, Bourdieu argues that social research cannot be objective because the social phenomenon itself is not objective. As there is no way for social scientists to provide an objective account of the practice, they should avoid imposing their views of actions and relationships, explained in terms of rules. Instead, they should focus on the relationships between people and their practices.

Language And Expression

The four chapters of *Outline* make a self-contained piece of work. The book's argument is logical and the text is written in a coherent way. However, the language and the structure of the sentences can be challenging. That has gained Bourdieu the reputation of being a notoriously difficult author to read.

Bourdieu described his style as "a permanent struggle against ordinary language," a struggle that resulted in the reader's own struggle to understand Bourdieu. In this respect, sociologist Richard Jenkins wrote: "Idiosyncratic usages and neologisms, allied to frequently repetitive, long sentences which are burdened down with a host of sub-clauses and discursive detours, combine with complicated diagrams and visual schemes to confront the reader with a task that many, whether they be undergraduates, postgraduates or professional social scientists, find daunting."[2]

Bourdieu's difficult language is an intentional choice. He insisted on challenging readers with their own ideas about the mechanisms that govern human action. Also, he invited them to question their presumptions about social theory in particular and the way they view the world in general.

More importantly, the theory that Bourdieu presents is actually not a theory in the conventional sense of the term. Rather than being constituted of abstract ideas, Bourdieu attempts to formulate a theory that is at the same time a description of practices. As practices are complex, he tries to convey this complexity in his language.

In addition, his writing style is intended to reflect the overall aim of the work. As the title says, the text is, indeed, an outline, not a conclusive and polished work, but rather tentative and open to revision. The reader should therefore feel legitimated to question his own as well as Bourdieu's definition of human action and other social phenomena.

NOTES

1 Pierre Bourdieu, *Outline of a Theory of Practice* (Cambridge: Cambridge University Press, 1977).

2 Richard Jenkins, *Pierre Bourdieu* (London: Routledge, 2014), 1.

SECONDARY IDEAS

KEY POINTS

- Bourdieu contends that human actions are practices determined by the interactions between the specific rules of the field, one's habitus and one's capital.

- Bourdieu's idea of "doxa" contributes to symbolic power embodied in various forms of capital.

- Although Bourdieu's ideas closely relate to issues of power struggles, they have been mostly overlooked in political science.

Other Ideas

The third chapter of *Outline of a Theory of Practice*, "Generative Schemes and Practical Logic: Invention Within Limits," focuses on the implications that Pierre Bourdieu's account of human action has for the social sciences. It contends that any account of social phenomena intending to develop an objective approach to the study and the theorization of practice is bound to fail.

In the final chapter of the book, "Structures, Habitus, Power: Basis for a Theory of Symbolic Power," Bourdieu introduces the role of capital as a relational force. He extends the definition of capital beyond its value in economic exchange. He introduces the forms of symbolic capital (cultural and social) in order to demonstrate how different types of capital can substitute economic capital and help actors in exercising power.

One's cultural capital depends on education and also on one's knowledge and intellectual abilities, which encourage one's advancement toward better social conditions. One's social capital depends on one's connections—that is, professional as well as personal

> ❝ To be able to see and describe the world as it is, you have to be ready to be always dealing with things that are complicated, confused, impure, uncertain, all of which runs counter to the usual idea of intellectual rigour. ❞
>
> Pierre Bourdieu, et al. *The Craft of Sociology: Epistemological Preliminaries*

networks. One's social and cultural capital is defined by the positions that actors occupy in the field. A field is the space that encompasses the choices available to agents, where these forms of capital can be converted into each other, including economic capital.

Finally, the notion of symbolic power is very important in Bourdieu's account, as it enables him to explain how some practices become unquestionable in a given society. It is symbolic power that helps actors to overcome the discrepancies between their beliefs and what challenges their beliefs, thereby maintaining the *status quo*.

In summary, human actions are practices determined by the interactions between the specific rules of the field, one's habitus and one's forms of capital. "In schematic form this has been expressed [(habitus) (capital)] + field = practice."[1] Importantly, habitus and field constantly interact and co-evolve in relation to each other. Therefore, any change in one implies a change in the other, although their potential alterations are minimized by the influence of symbolic power.

Exploring The Ideas

In addition to the concepts above, *Outline* introduces the concept of "doxa." This refers to situations in societies where, "what is essential goes without saying because it comes without saying: the tradition is silent, not least about itself as a tradition."[2] Doxa is undiscussable; that is, there is no room for dissidence. It is unanimous, and taken for granted. When it acts, it goes unnoticed and there is no questioning of legitimacy and power. As Bourdieu explains, "The adherence expressed in the doxic relation to the social world is the absolute form of recognition of legitimacy through misrecognition of arbitrariness, since it is unaware of the very question of legitimacy, which arises from competition for legitimacy, and hence from conflict between groups claiming to possess it."[3]

Bourdieu borrows the notion of doxa from an early work by Husserl.[4] However, his usage of the term "conceptualization of doxa" as a unanimous and unspoken aspect of social life is markedly different, for it closely relates to his discussion of symbolic power. Symbolic power uses doxa to replace visible and explicit forms of violence with invisible and implicit ones. In this way, symbolic power enables the establishment of categories that prevent actors from thinking in ways that could liberate them from their condition of subjugation. Later on, Bourdieu explains that doxa strengthens through the interactions between habitus and field, for each act in accordance with social conventions reinforces "the correspondence between the ... social structures and mental structures"[5] of the actors.

Although doxa remains undiscussed most of the time, its arbitrariness becomes evident when conflicts arise between dominant and dominated classes. When that happens, it slips into a space where agents are able to discuss and even question it. When doxa is questioned, a fracture in social order occurs that can potentially translate into social change. It follows that practice is not fixed, but changes through time under certain conditions. This change is not discussed in depth by Bourdieu, which is perhaps a limitation of his theory. Still, doxa is an important concept that researchers can use to examine the mechanisms that regulate social change.

Overlooked

Since *Outline* is a very important text in the social sciences, one can hardly find any aspect of it that has been overlooked. However, there are some aspects of the text that have been less discussed.

For example, political scientists have not benefited from the text as much as scholars in other branches of the social sciences. Bourdieu has stood outside the mainstream of political science, and *Outline* is not directly written to fit this discipline. Bourdieu hardly discusses political institutions, such as parties, states, and unions. However, for Bourdieu, political issues should not be understood as limited to the political sphere, but rather as connected to every aspect of social life.

Power, for instance, is an integral part of social relations that is reproduced in societies. Sociology, accordingly, includes the study of power dynamics. As such, for Bourdieu, there is no fundamental distinction between sociology and political science.

Three forms of power conceptualized by Bourdieu can be particularly useful in political science: a) power that is embodied in different forms of capital (e.g. cultural, social, etc.); b) power with regard to the struggles that actors have over the forms of capital (fields of power); and c) power that legitimizes doxa (shared values and beliefs) in the social sphere (symbolic power and violence).[6]

NOTES

1 Jessie Abrahams, Nicola Ingram, Jenny Thatcher, and Ciaran Burke, *Bourdieu: The Next Generation: The Development of Bourdieu's Intellectual Heritage in Contemporary UK Sociology* (London: Routledge), 3.

2 Pierre Bourdieu, *Outline of a Theory of Practice* (Cambridge: Cambridge University Press, 1977), 167.

3 Bourdieu, *Outline,* 168.

4 Edmund Husserl, *Experience and Judgement* (London: Routledge and Kegan Paul, 1973).

5 Bourdieu, *Outline*, 164.

6 David Swartz, "Pierre Bourdieu's Political Sociology and Public Sociology," in *Cultural analysis and Bourdieu's legacy: settling accounts and developing alternatives*, ed. Elizabeth Silva and Alan Warde (London: Routledge, 2010), 45–59.

ACHIEVEMENT

KEY POINTS

- Bourdieu has been criticized for failing to move beyond the intellectual traditions that he sought to transcend.

- The widespread impact of the book is due to subsequent English translations and the applicability of its main concepts.

- Although *Outline of a Theory of Practice* has been criticized for being limited to 1970s French society, its concepts have been applied throughout the social sciences.

Assessing The Argument

In *Outline of a Theory of Practice* Pierre Bourdieu attempted to move beyond structuralism by conceptualizing human action as conscious strategies rather than the mere result of internalized structures. However, it has been pointed out that since these strategies are influenced by behavioral patterns that the actor has internalized, such patterns pre-exist the actor. Just as, according to structuralism, actors are not aware of the influence of the structures, the Bourdieusian actor is not aware of his own dispositions. It looks like structures and habitus are not as different as Bourdieu has attempted to show. It is therefore legitimate to criticize Bourdieu's attempt to move beyond structuralism, for it could be argued that he has merely replaced structure with habitus without really changing its function in determining social action.

That is not to say that Bourdieu's argument is devoid of value. As one of his critics wrote, "Bourdieu has gone some way beyond structuralism."[1] However, Bourdieu has also maintained some of the

> **❝** In the best French tradition he has presented a tantalizing menu of intellectual dishes combining new and old concepts prepared in new ways, all flavoured by a heavy sauce of heartily unintelligible prose that at times seems to mask and hence deny the savour promised by the initial aromatic programme. **❞**
>
> Gregory Acciaioli, *Knowing What You're Doing*

features for which structuralism was criticized, such as the inability to explain how behaviors can change if norms and rules, or structures, remain the same. Hence, the book may well appear as a re-edition of the objectivist approach, as it has been considered by some of its critics. In this respect, his translator Richard Nice wrote, "The fact remains that a text which seeks to break out of a scheme of thought as deeply embedded as the opposition between subjectivism and objectivism is fated to be perceived through the categories which it seeks to transcend."[2]

However, the insights that the text brings are thought-provoking, but the richness and the depth of the concepts introduced in the text demand an attentive and patient reader. If the reader is not prepared to work their way through the complexity of the text, the value of its concepts might remain mostly inaccessible.

Achievement In Context

In this book, Bourdieu's intention was to make a dialogue with anthropologists and sociologists, as opposed to scholars from other disciplines. However, *Outline* has turned out to be a book about the theory of action more generally. As such, the audience it reached was beyond the original intentions of the author and the book became relevant to a much broader range of social scientists.

Its widespread diffusion depended also on the translations that became available at different points in time. The French version of the book was published in 1972 and titled *Esquisse d'une Theorie de la Pratique*. The first English version appeared in 1977. It not only offered a translation of the book, but it also advanced and refined Bourdieu's arguments set in the original French version, although some ethnographic parts were curtailed for reasons of space.

Initially, Bourdieu's work was not widely known. Then, when more translations of his work became available during the 80s and 90s, its popularity grew. Outside France, anthropologists and sociologists of education became more familiar with the work. However, it was only a few years after *Outline*'s publication in English that the book became very popular among social scientists.

Another reason behind the achievements of *Outline* is the great importance of structuralism at the time of its publication and, on the other hand, the value of the ethnographic method. Structuralism was extremely popular because it sought to provide scientific answers to deep humanistic questions. Bourdieu, however, could not apply structuralist schemes to his ethnographic material, thereby exposing the limits of a very popular theory at the time. Hence, *Outline* cast light on a more general and controversial problem in social sciences, that of imposing the researcher's perspective upon the views of his research subjects, thereby treating them as objects.

Limitations

One of the criticisms of Bourdieu's work in general was its limitedness to French society of the time. In particular, Bourdieu was inspired by some characteristics of contemporary French culture. For example, his conceptualization of symbolic power and cultural capital was inspired by his interest in the cultural and socio-economic stratification of French society.

On the other hand, the applicability Bourdieu's theory might be limited because of its many constituents, such as capital, field, and habitus. They are closely interwoven, which means that they can hardly be used in isolation. As a consequence, applying them separately to fit the specificities of other contexts, such as the USA, might be difficult. However, scholars can still attempt to apply them to different empirical contexts by tailoring them to specific research needs.

Over the last two decades, this attempt to apply Bourdieu's theory beyond its immediate context is reflected in the increasing number of citations of *Outline* in American journals.[3] American sociologists such as Neil Fligstein* and Michèle Lamont* have adapted Bourdieu's theory to specific empirical contexts of their research. Similarly, a group of researchers demonstrated that a form of capitalism could emerge in postcommunist Central Europe because holders of cultural capital, a concept borrowed from Bourdieu, used their knowledge rather than their material assets.[4]

Another limitation is, perhaps, the difficult language used in the book. Bourdieu presents his challenging concepts in lengthy sentences with a complex structure and vocabulary. This complexity has inevitably given rise to diversified understandings, interpretations, and applications of the text. The concepts of habitus, field, capital, and practice have appealed to social scientists in different fields who used them differently, depending on their individual needs and research contexts. Although such a diversity of applications might suggest that Bourdieu has sometimes been misunderstood,[5] the flexibility of *Outline* has contributed to its widespread diffusion across different disciplines.

NOTES

1   Richard Jenkins, *Pierre Bourdieu* (London: Routledge, 2014), 20.

2   Richard Nice, Translator's Foreword to *Outline of a Theory of Practice* by Pierre Bourdieu (Cambridge: Cambridge University Press, 1977), viii.

3   Jeffrey J. Sallaz and Jane Zavisca, "Bourdieu in American Sociology, 1980–2004," *Annual Review of Sociology* 33.1 (2007).

4   Gil, Eyal, Iván Szelényi, and Eleanor R. Townsley, *Making capitalism without capitalists: Class formation and elite struggles in post-communist Central Europe* (London: Verso, 1998), 74.

5   Nicolas Truong and Nicolas Weill, "A decade after his death, French sociologist Pierre Bourdieu stands tall," *Guardian* 2012. Accessed July 19, 2017 https://www.theguardian.com/world/2012/feb/21/pierre-bourdieu-philosophy-most-quoted.

MODULE 8
PLACE IN THE AUTHOR'S WORK

KEY POINTS

- *Outline of a Theory of Practice* is Bourdieu's first attempt to systematize his thought based on his ethnography of the Kabyle people.

- *Outline* illustrates Bourdieu's practice theory, although some of its main concepts can be found in his earlier, as well as his later books.

- The significance of *Outline* lies mainly in the impact it had on social sciences with concepts that Bourdieu continued developing throughout his career.

Positioning

Outline of a Theory of Practice is significant in Pierre Bourdieu's overall intellectual life in at least three major respects.

First, the work results from a major intellectual turning point in the life of the author, namely Bourdieu's experience in Algeria. He left France in 1956 as a soldier and a philosopher and he returned in 1960 as an ethnographer and social anthropologist. The material he collected was to be published in a number of books and articles across several decades. *Outline* is just one of these.

Second, the significance of *Outline* rests in it being the first attempt by its author to systematize his thoughts. As such, this book is a fundamental milestone in Bourdieu's career. In *Outline* he sketched the theory that was to be presented even more systematically in *The Logic of Practice*,[1] which was published in 1992. Although Bourdieu continued to develop his concepts throughout his career, he did not substantially alter the fundamental tenets of his theory of practice.

> ❝ This text is the cornerstone of an oeuvre which encompasses numerous major works in both anthropology and sociology—which crosses and challenges the boundary dividing their objects, tasks, and theories, and forces attention to the social conditions in which such sciences are possible. ❞
>
> Richard Nice, "Translator's Foreword," *Outline of a Theory of Practice*

However, it is possible to identify elements of Bourdieu's intellectual work, both before and after *Outline*, that can provide a deeper and more subtle understanding of the concepts first presented in the text. For example, in "System of Education and System of Thought,"[2] published in English in 1967, he illustrated how the way actors classify and categorize social reality is impressed upon them by means of schooling, that is, a structured institution. This was an initial attempt to conceptualize social domination, which in *Outline* he elaborates more systematically in the concept of symbolic power.

Outline is, moreover, one of the first of Bourdieu's publications that was translated into English. It was thanks to this translation that the book has become so widespread. However, it should be noted that the English version was more than a translation, as it considerably refined and expanded the original content.

Integration

Outline presents the foundations of Bourdieu's theory of practice. He enhanced and enriched the ideas presented in *Outline* in his 1992 book, *The Logic of Practice.* However, he did not modify the fundamental ideas of the text in this later work. Therefore, while the understanding of the theory should refer to *Outline*, it is possible to find other illustrations of the same ideas in earlier as well as later books.

For example, the idea of a discrepancy between structure and agency already appeared in Bourdieu's 1960 ethnography among the farmers of the Béarn* in south-western France. Just like in the Kabyle ethnography, the case material used to discuss the inadequacy of abstract theories was provided by kinship norms.[3] The local norms in Béarn dictated that land was to be inherited by the eldest son and that younger siblings received compensation for giving up any claim to that land. In practice, however, the head of the household interpreted and applied the rules according to contextual priorities and in the form of strategies that could not be subsumed in an a-temporal, general, and formalized law.

Another discussion of the same concept is found in Bourdieu's study of honor among the Kabyle people, which Bourdieu first published in 1965. Kabyle men do not, he argued, earn or lose honor by simply abiding by or neglecting pre-existing norms. They do so by means of a game of challenge and counter-challenge and material transactions carried out over a long period of time. Bourdieu's interest in Kabyle honor was but a precursor of his later studies on the pursuit and social recognition of symbolic power.

Even though *Outline* counts as a first effort to systematize Bourdieu's theory of practice, some of its concepts were further developed later. In particular, one of the important aspects of Bourdieu's work, field, was less developed in this book, in which a large portion of the text was devoted to habitus. The notion of field was elaborated in more detail in his subsequent works.

Significance

Outline provided the social sciences with an innovative epistemological and methodological framework. Also, Bourdieu's theory offered a new way of thinking about social reality more generally. He conceived of social phenomena as inseparable from practice. This practice-oriented way of thinking about social reality has shaped the social sciences, as has the concept of habitus.

This can be traced back to Bourdieu's early work on Béarn farmers, where he used the concept of habitus to explain their actions.[4] In *The Inheritors*,[5] Bourdieu used another term, habitat. This concept was intended to explain how different social classes were differently equipped to access university education. It was in *Outline* that Bourdieu formally introduced habitus for the first time. The concept was so important that it became a fundamental component of his work throughout his entire career.

The same can be said about other aspects of his work. Although Bourdieu published in various disciplines and areas in social sciences, ranging from cultural studies to arts and education, these publications maintained the epistemological and methodological position presented in *Outline*. As has been suggested by one of his admirers, there is not such a significant difference between the later Bourdieu and the early Bourdieu.[6]

NOTES

1   Pierre Bourdieu, *The Logic of Practice* (Stanford: Stanford University Press, 1992).

2   Pierre Bourdieu, "System of Education and System of Thought," *International Social Science Journal,* XIX.3 (1967): 338–58.

3   Pierre Bourdieu, *In other words: Essays towards a reflexive sociology* (Stanford: Stanford University Press, 1990), 59–61.

4   Pierre Bourdieu, "Célibat et condition paysanne," Études rurales, no. 5/6 (1962).

5   Pierre Bourdieu and Jean Claude Passeron, *The Inheritors: French Students and Their Relation to Culture* (Chicago: University of Chicago Press, 1979).

6   Marcel Fournier, "Reflections on the Legacy of Pierre Bourdieu," *The Canadian Journal of Sociology/Cahiers canadiens de sociologie* 27.4 (2002).

SECTION 3
IMPACT

MODULE 9
THE FIRST RESPONSES

KEY POINTS

- Bourdieu has been criticized for failing to overcome objectivism, providing a tautological* definition of habitus, and for writing in an intellectualist fashion.

- Bourdieu recognized the risk of circularity in the concept of habitus, and responded to the criticism concerning the problem of change.

- The current trend among some researchers is to use Bourdieu's theory critically rather than blindly applying his concepts and intellectual style.

Criticism

The criticisms of *Outline of a Theory of Practice* encompass a number of aspects. Perhaps, the most persuasive critiques relate to the following two aspects.

First, the claim that Pierre Bourdieu makes with respect to his theory as non-objectivist.[1] Although in *Outline* Bourdieu attacks the objectivism of much of contemporary social sciences and claims that his alternative is not objectivist, critics have stated that he fails to deliver on this premise.[2] They have argued that Bourdieu's refutation of objective–subjective dualism does not really lead to his introduction of a third way. For them, he remains an objectivist, albeit a sophisticated one. They claim that the notion of habitus, which is supposed to be an alternative to the objective–subjective dichotomy,* in fact reproduces the objectivist research program, although in a very complex way. It is an individual and isolated

> ❝ Bourdieu does not really resolve the issue of the locus of habitus, for he sometimes situates habitus in the individual agent, yet sometimes refers to it as a product of history that determines both individual and collective practices. ❞
>
> Gregory Acciaioli, *Knowing What You're Doing*

mechanism, which does not correspond with the practice approach as a relational concept that Bourdieu had promised to his audience.

Second, critics argued that if habitus is to be realized as a relational concept, it needs to be distinguished from the practices that it generates. This, in turn, requires a detailed explanation of the internal mechanisms of habitus, which is absent in Bourdieu's work. For example, considering one's habitus as industrious because one produces considerable output is tautological. It does not provide any insight into how practices are triggered in reality, although it may provoke thinking.[3]

A third, milder, criticism relates to the intellectualist nature of Bourdieu's work.[4] From the outset, Bourdieu objects to the abstract nature of academic inquiry in its current form. Academics, he claims, fail to represent the mystery of practice. He thus calls for not only a *theory of practice*, but also a theory that has to be *practical*. However, as he himself acknowledges,[5] his language is often too intellectualist and difficult to access, even for the specialists in his own field.

Responses

In response to the critics who questioned the usefulness of the concept of habitus, considering it a tautology, Bourdieu asserts that he is fully aware of the danger involved in the conceptual circularity of habitus.[6] Saying that someone makes petty bourgeois choices because he has a petty bourgeois habitus is circular reasoning. However, he provides no conceptual answer to this problem. Acknowledgment of this problem does not obviate the chances of circularity.[7]

Concerning the objectivist nature of the concept of habitus, critics have argued that the theory of practice championed by Bourdieu does not explain how change is enacted while it favors the reproduction mechanisms of social order. Hence, habitus appears to be a mechanism that can explain continuity more than change. If actors cumulatively carry their past and embody their habitus as unconsciously internalized dispositions, then social change is seen as impossible. As a consequence, a lack of attention to the mechanisms of social change is one of the most commonly mentioned critiques of *Outline* as fundamentally deterministic.*

Bourdieu responded to this criticism in three ways. First, he argued that the habitus is not as devoid of choice as represented by his critics, although the range of choices and attitudes are influenced and, to a certain extent, limited by social structures.[8] Second, social actors have aspirations and expectations that can transform the habitus and the practices it enacts. Third, the habitus can be consciously controlled by means of one's reflexive awakening to the workings of human societies.

Conflict And Consensus

In his first years in French academia, Bourdieu inspired mixed reactions from his rivals in sociology and some have even accused him of being dismissive and arrogant.[9] This partly relates to the nature of the country's academic environment, that is its fractured intellectual islands with adversaries and competitors. As Bourdieu's work has been always contested in French academia, no account of its success history is complete without considering the personal tensions of his time.[10] The international responses to Bourdieu have been mainly intellectual; however, in France, mixed emotions continue to persist.

Recent contributions in the social sciences have moved to viewing Bourdieu as a reference point. The current trend among some researchers, such as those in the Bourdieu Study Group, is to *think with* Bourdieu, but not to blindly stick to his ideas and framework. Moreover, researchers have made attempts to focus on the areas that Bourdieu has overlooked or ignored because they did not fit within his framework. Thus, the consensus is to read Bourdieu *without* Bourdieu.[11]

In order to explain this consensus, it is necessary to understand what it is that scholars found most useful in Bourdieu's theory. That is only possible by taking a more nuanced understanding of the text. Rather than looking for a definitive answer to the question whether Bourdieu got his theory right or not, the readers should accept that sometimes academic debates fade with time. In other words, rather than taking sides in the structure/agency debate, they should build upon the skills they develop by engaging with the debate itself.

NOTES

1   Gregory L. Acciaioli, "Knowing what you're doing: A Review of Pierre Bourdieu's Outline of a Theory of Practice." *Canberra Anthropology* 4.1 (1981): 44.

2   Richard Jenkins, *Pierre Bourdieu* (London: Routledge, 2014), 47.

3   Roy Nash. "Bourdieu, 'habitus', and educational research: Is it all worth the candle?" *British Journal of Sociology of Education* 20.2 (1999): 175–187.

4   Jenkins, *Pierre Bourdieu*, 1.

5   Pierre Bourdieu, *Outline of a Theory of Practice* (Cambridge: Cambridge University Press, 1977), 116–117.

6   Pierre Bourdieu and Loïc J.D. Wacquant, (eds.) *An Invitation to Reflexive Sociology* (Cambridge Polity Press, 1992), 192.

7   Karl Maton, "Habitus," in *Pierre Bourdieu: Key Concepts,* edited by Michael Grenfell (Durham: Acumen, 2008), 62.

8   Pierre Bourdieu and Loïc J.D. Wacquant, "The purpose of reflexive sociology (The Chicago Workshop)", in *An Invitation to Reflexive Sociology*, edited by Pierre Bourdieu and Loïc J.D. Wacquant (Cambridge Polity Press, 1992), 61–216.

9   Pekka Sulkunen, "Society made visible – on the cultural sociology of Pierre
    Bourdieu." *Acta Sociologica* 25.2 (1982): 106. See also Marie-Anne Lescourret,
    Bourdieu (Paris: Flammarion, 2008).

10 Elizabeth Silva and Alan Warde, "Introduction: the importance of Bourdieu,"
    in *Cultural analysis and Bourdieu's legacy: settling accounts and developing
    alternatives*, edited by Elizabeth Silva and Alan Warde (London: Routledge, 2010).

11 Michael Grenfell, "Working with habitus and field: the logic of Bourdieu's
    practice," in *Cultural analysis and Bourdieu's legacy: settling accounts and
    developing alternatives*, edited by Elizabeth Silva and Alan Warde (London:
    Routledge, 2010), 14–27.

MODULE 10
THE EVOLVING DEBATE

KEY POINTS

* *Outline of a Theory of Practice* has been criticized, but the concepts it advanced have been widely applied.

* Rather than creating Bourdieusian schools, scholars applied and adapted Bourdieu's concepts in different ways depending on time and place.

* The application of Bourdieu's theory is widespread in the social sciences, although this sometimes reflects a shallow engagement with it.

Uses And Problems

The concepts that Pierre Bourdieu presented in *Outline of a Theory of Practice* have been widely used in the social sciences and beyond, although they have been criticized by some scholars for a variety of reasons.

Concerning the uses, over the past three decades Bourdieu's theoretical and methodological insights have contributed to the development of the social sciences as a whole. His critique of structuralism first had a profound impact on French ethnology, and then on anthropology more generally. His discussion of the epistemological limits of social research called for a much more reflexive position on the part of the researchers, which has since shaped social sciences in new, less objectivist ways. For example, although Lévi-Strauss's theories are still very important in anthropology, after Bourdieu it has become necessary to take a rather nuanced approach to structuralism.

66 The key problem is that, as Bourdieu is increasingly the 'go to' theorist, his concepts are used without the necessary theoretical consideration or empirical reflection required for a rich and nuanced conceptual tool such as habitus, resulting in an under-theorised position. 99

Ciaran Burke, *Bourdieu's theory of practice: maintaining the role of capital*

As for the problems in *Outline*, the most significant critiques of Bourdieu's work lie in the difficulties associated with the notion of habitus.[1] Evidently, as the pillar of the practice theory, inevitably, the concept of habitus is heavily burdened with intellectual and practical implications, making it vulnerable to criticism. For example, the concept has been criticized as homogenizing the diversity of groups as if actors belonged to a closed system of dispositions. In such a homogeneous and impermeable system change is not possible, for habitus simply reproduces itself.[2]

Although Bourdieu continued to develop, revise, and refine his theory throughout the rest of his life, he never reconsidered the substance of his concepts. In particular, the 1992 book *The Logic of Practice* suggests a significant development of the theory with a focus on the notion of time. As a consequence, Bourdieu's theory of practice has been widely used despite its problems.

Schools Of Thought

Concerning the followers of Bourdieu, the sociologist Jean-Claude Passeron* said that his theories were "likely, particularly due to the force of his most ambitious concepts, to encourage novices to indulge in sterile, mechanical imitation."[3] That might have happened in the early years since the publication of Bourdieu's first books. However, followers have also developed their own versions of Bourdieu's theories, with particular developments in different academic fields and different countries.

In France, for example, Luc Boltanski* was a disciple of Bourdieu, but later he distanced himself from the hermeneutics of suspicion* that Bourdieu inherited from Marx. While Bourdieu's method was to understand practices through an analysis of habitus that drew heavily on the actors' past experiences, Boltanski looks at practices as much more of a product of free will. Actors, for Boltanski, can understand their own motivations. They are aware of their habitus, rather than just blindly motivated by it.

In Britain, Bourdieu's work has been particularly influential in the development of the sociology of education, especially with the book *Reproduction in Education, Society and Culture*.[4] Recently, there has been an enthusiastic return to Bourdieu with the establishment of the British Sociological Association's Bourdieu Study Group in 2012. Although these scholars investigate phenomena more than 40 years after the first publication of *Outline*, they still find Bourdieu's ideas useful for their work.

In the United States, scholars trained in the Bourdieusian tradition, such as Loïc Wacquant,* encouraged the diffusion of Bourdieu's ideas, reflected in the growing number of citations between 1980 and 2004.[5]

In Current Scholarship

In current scholarship, Bourdieu's work is used by sociologists and anthropologists, but also by scholars in education and international relations. Bourdieu's theory of practice has been applied to themes as diverse as research on education,[6] the formation of socio-cultural identities,[7] and gender studies.[8]

However, Reay argued that such a widespread application often does not reflect a deep engagement with the original theory, but rather a mere point of reference.[9] Recently, the Bourdieu Study Group addressed this problem throughout a thorough reflection on the original tenets of Bourdieu's theory of practice. Its members applied Bourdieu's ideas to problems that Bourdieu himself addressed, "such as social mobility, social class and political transformations"[10] as well as ones he was not necessarily concerned with, such as migration, "race"/ethnicity, and gender. The result has been the publishing of *Bourdieu: The Next Generation* in 2016, which illustrates how "Bourdieu's intellectual heritage is being developed in UK sociology through the work of a new generation of Bourdieusian scholars."[11]

In addition to disciplines that have been historical recipients of Bourdieu's theories, such as sociology and anthropology, interest for Bourdieu has recently developed in unexpected disciplines. For example, one international relations (IR) scholar recently wrote: "Bourdieu helps us rediscover the everyday practices, symbolic structures and arenas of conflict that bring many other actors into perspective, rather than just focusing on nation states that produce (what we call) international politics. An engagement with his work redirects our discipline from being influenced by overly abstracted and simplified reifications of world politics, which is currently the case in both positivist* and post-positivist* IR schools."[12]

NOTES

1   Anthony King, "Thinking with Bourdieu against Bourdieu: A 'practical' critique of the habitus." *Sociological Theory* 18.3 (2000): 417–433.

2   Karl Maton, "Habitus," in *Pierre Bourdieu: Key Concepts,* edited by Michael Grenfell (Durham: Acumen, 2008), 62.

3   Nicolas Truong and Nicolas Weill, "A decade after his death, French sociologist Pierre Bourdieu stands tall," *Guardian* 2012. Accessed July 19, 2017. https://www.theguardian.com/world/2012/feb/21/pierre-bourdieu-philosophy-most-quoted.

4   Pierre Bourdieu and Jean-Claude Passeron, *Reproduction in education, society and culture* (Thousand Oaks, CA, US: Sage) 1990.

5   Jeffrey J. Sallaz and Jane Zavisca, "Bourdieu in American Sociology, 1980–2004," *Annual Review of Sociology* 33.1 (2007).

6   Diane Reay, Miriam E. David, and Stephen J. Ball, *Degrees of choice: Class, race, gender and higher education* (Sterling, US: Trentham Books, 2005); Nicola Ingram, "Working-class boys, educational success and the misrecognition of working-class culture." *British Journal of Sociology of Education* 30.4 (2009), 421–434; Harriet Bradley and Nicola Ingram, "Banking on the future: Choices, aspirations and economic hardship in working-class student experience." *Class inequality in austerity Britain* (London: Palgrave Macmillan, 2013), 51–69.

7   Catherine F. Schryer and Philippa Spoel, "Genre theory, health-care discourse, and professional identity formation." *Journal of Business and Technical Communication* 19.3 (2005), 249–278.

8   Lisa Adkins and Beverley Skeggs, (eds.) *Feminism after Bourdieu* (Oxford: Blackwell, 2004).

9   Diane Reay *et al., Degrees of choice: Class, race, gender and higher education.*

10 Jessie Abrahams, Nicola Ingram, Jenny Thatcher, and Ciaran Burke, *Bourdieu: The Next Generation: The Development of Bourdieu's Intellectual Heritage in Contemporary UK Sociology* (London: Routledge), 4.

11 Abrahams *et al., Bourdieu: The Next Generation,* 1.

12 Rebecca Adler-Nissen, (ed.) *Bourdieu in International Relations: Rethinking key concepts in IR*. (London: Routledge, 2012), 1.

MODULE 11
IMPACT AND INFLUENCE TODAY

KEY POINTS

- The text is significant and widely cited in the contemporary social sciences.

- The text challenges objectivist/subjectivist accounts of social action.

- Even the opponents of the text believe that Bourdieu's concepts can be useful to analyze and study phenomena in different contexts.

Position

Outline of a Theory of Practice centers on the fundamental question of human action and how it is determined. This is not only an important question, but is also at the core of any social theory. However, *Outline* did not achieve the immediate fame that *Distinction*[1] did. Its success was gradual.

In France, Pierre Bourdieu was an important scholar when he wrote *Outline*; however, he did not become internationally known until the 1990s, when many of his contributions were translated into English. In order to understand this corpus of publications, then, researchers returned to *Outline* to discuss the general theory of practice that Bourdieu advocated.

At that point, the impact of the text on its intellectual context was massive. It has since influenced those researchers who have focused on analyzing the links between socio-cultural structures and human actions. Therefore, its major influence lies in integrating culture into social analysis.

> **❝ From the principle of mutual recognition of equality in honour there follows a first corollary: the challenge confers honour. 'The man who has no enemies', say the Kabyles, 'is a donkey' (the symbol of passivity). There is nothing worse than to pass unnoticed. ❞**
>
> Pierre Bourdieu, *Outline of a Theory of Practice*

Initially, the text addressed sociology and anthropology.[2] However, gradually, it started diffusing and finding new audiences among other social scientists. Bourdieu was active in many fields, such as anthropology, sociology, and cultural education. In addition, *Outline* had the potential to be applied to other fields in the social sciences.

Consequently, the reach of *Outline* did not stop there and extended to other domains, such as management and organizational studies. The initial encounter of management scholars with the text was mediated by educational researchers.[3] The growing number of citations of *Outline* (almost 40,000 according to Google Scholar at the time of writing this analysis) demonstrates the reach and significance of the work in the contemporary social sciences.

Interaction

The theory advanced in *Outline* inspired one of the dominant streams of contemporary sociology, which challenges the approaches that favor either structure or agency. It challenges, in other words, the approaches that explicitly or implicitly try to explain social actions through structural properties (e.g. social norms, contracts, values, etc.) as well as those that explain social action as resulting from individual will and opportunistic behavior.

It has been argued, however, that this approach to human action should not be objectified. That is, scholars should not understand the theory of practice as a mere middle ground between structure and agency. The point of the book is also to unsettle its readers through confusing, frustrating, and enlightening them.[4]

Two contemporary approaches are developed in response to the blind followers of Bourdieu's theory. The first one is the Actor Network Theory (ANT) created by French scholars Bruno Latour and Michel Callon, who assert that agency is not only embodied in humans; non-humans (such as artifacts) can also have agency. The other approach developed at the *Groupe de Sociologie Politique et Morale*, and founded by Boltanski, explores the actors' perspectives in social life assuming that they have more agency than they do in Bourdieu's theory.

Moreover, *Outline* interacts with the quantitative approach dominant in American sociology. For example, the concept of cultural capital has been used in a quantitative study of high school grades to demonstrate the influence of family background on student performance.[5] In addition, Bourdieu's introduction of different forms of capital suggests that they can be converted from one to another. That has promoted a much more flexible definition of what capital is. As a consequence of this interaction, the different concepts of capital have been developed and applied in various ways in different branches of the social sciences and beyond.

The Continuing Debate
The debate around the text has spread in various directions. *Outline* divides its readers as different scholars have different takes on the theory. Although some tend to follow Bourdieu's methods and approach with a high degree of loyalty, most prefer to challenge his underlying assumptions and modify them in order to apply them to different contexts.

The charge of objectivism perhaps limits the application of Bourdieu's theory more than any criticism. On the other hand, since

Bourdieu, it has become increasingly difficult for scholars to belong to either subjectivism or objectivism. In that sense, Bourdieu's attempt to move beyond these two broadly defined ways of thinking, has been achieved.

For example, American sociology was challenged by *Outline* for its predominant use of survey methods. These methods were in opposition to the engaging approach that Bourdieu proposed, for they emphasized the objectivity of statistical results and undermined individual perspectives. Despite this difference, though, some American sociologists embraced Bourdieu's framework and critically worked with the French sociologist.[6]

In a similar vein, researchers from different disciplines have approached and contested *Outline* in different ways. Eventually, however, they have modified and adopted to their contexts. For example, various specialties in sociology, including organization sociology, poverty, immigration, economic sociology,*and gender studies* have adopted a Bourdieusian framework as a central approach to their studies. New fields, such as cultural sociology, constitute a wider move labeled as "cultural turn" in sociological studies over the past two decades.[7] "Cultural turn" refers to the wide range of topics discussed by the sociologists that put culture at the center of their analysis as Bourdieu did in *Outline*, as well as in his other contributions.

Bourdieu's theory has been an endless source of debates, controversies, and critiques and has been highly contested. However, regardless of the opinion of his critics, Bourdieu is generally considered as *good to think with*,[8] and his contribution to the field of sociology should be celebrated.

NOTES

1   Pierre Bourdieu, *Distinction: A Social Critique of the Judgment of Taste* (Harvard: Harvard University Press, 1984).

2   Michael Grenfell, *Pierre Bourdieu: Key Concepts* (Durham: Acumen, 2008), 1.

3   Jean Lave and Etienne Wenger, *Situated learning: Legitimate peripheral participation* (Cambridge: Cambridge University Press, 1991).

4   Paul Michael Garrett, "The Relevance of Bourdieu for Social Work: A Reflection on Obstacles and Omissions," *Journal of Social Work* 7.3 (2007).

5   Paul DiMaggio, "Cultural capital and school success: The impact of status culture participation on the grades of US high school students." *American Sociological Review* 47.2 (1982).

6   Jeffrey J. Sallaz and Jane Zavisca, "Bourdieu in American Sociology, 1980–2004," *Annual Review of Sociology* 33.1 (2007).

7   Michèle Lamont, "How has Bourdieu been good to think with? The case of the United States." *Sociological Forum*. 27.1 (Blackwell Publishing Ltd, 2012).

8   Michael Grenfell, "Working with habitus and field: the logic of Bourdieu's practice," in *Cultural Analysis and Bourdieu's Legacy: Settling Accounts and Developing Alternatives,* edited by Elizabeth Silva and Alan Warde (London, UK: Routledge, 2010).

MODULE 12
WHERE NEXT?

KEY POINTS

- Although *Outline of a Theory of Practice* has been widely studied, there is room for deepening our understanding of its concepts.

- The conceptual toolkit formulated by Bourdieu will continue to be applied to various contemporary research questions.

- *Outline* has shaped the social sciences, it still bears considerable influence, and future researchers will continue to apply its concepts.

Potential

Although *Outline of a Theory of Practice* has been widely studied and discussed, it has the potential for further exploration. Equally, while habitus has been studied much more than other concepts, such as field and capital, there is always room for deepening our understanding of the concept.

For example, the cognitive roots of the concept of habitus deserve further attention in sociology. Pierre Bourdieu talks about the conscious and unconscious aspects of habitus, but he never goes into depth in discussing their dynamics and mechanisms.

Furthermore, Omar Lizardo* argues that although Bourdieu's introduction of the notion of habitus is mainly discussed in a sociological context, it has significant intersections with the cognitive theory of Jean Piaget.*[1] Therefore, it is important to both consider these cognitive roots and further develop them in relation to habitus.

In fact, for many, habitus is still a mysterious concept in Bourdieu's framework, and unraveling its cognitive foundations can significantly

> **❝**Bourdieu is … enormously good to think with. … If one makes the initial effort, it is … impossible to remain neutral about what he is saying. … He raises tricky questions and helps to provide some of the means by which they may be answered. Bourdieu's work offers the patient reader a tremendously useful intellectual resource. **❞**
>
> Richard Jenkins, *Pierre Bourdieu*

add to our understanding about its nature. One of the benefits of exploring and advancing the cognitive aspect of habitus is that such an exploration might discourage attacks on habitus as an objectivist and reductionist concept.

Reconsidering and reinterpreting *Outline* in the light of the discussed points can, thus, enhance and enrich our understanding of the text, and may assist social scientists to go beyond Bourdieu. Exposing the fundamental concepts of the text to new interpretations and examining them with the tools of other disciplines can contribute to extending and refining the type of social theory that Bourdieu advocated.

Future Directions

Outline is not only relevant today, but it is increasingly receiving attention from scholars all over the world. Currently, there are not many rival theories that can easily replace Bourdieu's framework. Even recent accounts in social theory like structuration,* which does not prioritize either structure or agency,[2] have their roots in Bourdieu's rejection of sociological dichotomies. Hence, it is reasonable to predict that, in the years to come, Bourdieu's theory of practice will continue to exert considerable influence in the social sciences and beyond.

Some have written about a "comeback" of Bourdieu across the

social sciences and the arts.[3] After slightly losing its edge during the 1990s, over the past 5–6 years there has been a new wave of PhD students who have appropriated Bourdieu's work in their studies. If these early research directions continue into the future, many sociologists in the United Kingdom will apply Bourdieu to new research questions. The recent activities of the Bourdieu Study Group seem to point in that direction.

For example, during her PhD, British sociologist Dr. Lisa Mckenzie applied Bourdieu to the ethnographic study of economic disadvantage in a council estate* in England. That has revealed how its residents are designated by the wider society as lacking particular forms of capital, a form of symbolic violence. Although her work also developed in other directions, Mckenzie still maintains an interest in Bourdieu, particularly with regard to the concept of capital in its different forms.

To take another example, Dr. Sam Friedman, a sociologist at the London School of Economics, applied the concept of different forms of capital to his doctoral research on inequality in the British school system. This interest has evolved into a number of research projects that have looked at inequalities in other dimensions of British society, such as the pay gap between employees from a working-class background and those from a more privileged upbringing. These research interests reveal a commitment to social justice, which can also be found in Bourdieu's work.

Summary

Pierre Bourdieu wrote *Outline of a Theory of Practice* on the basis of his ethnographic observations during the colonial war in Algeria. His data did not fit into the two prominent theoretical approaches in the social sciences of the time, namely structuralism and existentialism. His theory of practice was an attempt to transcend the opposition between these approaches by means of a new set of concepts, including habitus, field, and various forms of capital.

Bourdieu's theory of practice broke with the past because it offered an alternative to the objectification of culture inherent in structuralism. On the other hand, it was not restricted by the epistemological limits of conventional ethnography. Rather than insisting on structural regularities or unfathomable free will, Bourdieu posited the habitus of actors as a system of dispositions operating in a field where various forms of capital are exchanged.

During the 40 years since the publication of *Outline*, this theory has attracted the interest, as well as the criticism, of many scholars. While Bourdieu never substantially altered the main tenets of his theory, his followers have adopted his concepts critically. The theory of practice has been prolifically applied in sociology and anthropology, but also in other related disciplines, such as educational research and international relations. In the future, it is reasonable to expect that it will be applied to the study of inequality, thanks to the longevity of its concepts and its continued relevance in social justice.

It has been argued that the success of this theory rests less in its content and more in its capacity to provoke new thinking. While the content has been severely criticized, academics from various fields continue to find inspiration from *Outline*. Rather than testing its validity, readers should understand its value to the social sciences over the last 40 years, which would have not been the same without *Outline of a Theory of Practice*.

NOTES

1   Omar Lizardo, "The cognitive origins of Bourdieu's habitus," *Journal for the Theory of Social Behaviour* 34.4 (2004).

2   Anthony Giddens, *The constitution of society: Outline of a theory of structuration* (Cambridge: Polity Press, 1984).

3   Nicola Truong and Nicolas Weill, "A decade after his death, French sociologist Pierre Bourdieu stands tall," *Guardian* 2012. Accessed July 19, 2017. https://www.theguardian.com/world/2012/feb/21/pierre-bourdieu-philosophy-most-quoted

GLOSSARY

GLOSSARY OF TERMS

Agency: the ability of individual social actors to decide how to act—the opposite of structure in the terminology of social sciences. Bourdieu argues that agency is accounted for in his theory of practice, but only as long as it is limited in patterns of dispositions.

Algerian War of Independence: an armed conflict between France and the Algerian Liberation Front that started in 1954 and ended in 1962 with the victory of the latter and the achievement of independence. Realizing the gap between the way French intellectuals understood the war and his own experiences, Bourdieu began writing about Algeria from within.

Alienation: a concept associated with Karl Marx that refers to the process by which the worker is made to feel disconnected from the products of their labor.

Anthropology: literally, the study of humankind, which can be subdivided into social, cultural, and physical anthropology. Bourdieu was particularly influential in anthropology thanks to his theory of practice that openly challenged the structuralist approach so prevalent in the anthropology of the mid-twentieth century.

Béarn: a French province in southwest France, located in the Pyrenees mountains on the border with Spain. It is the rural area where Bourdieu was brought up.

Binary opposition: a pair of individual elements related by virtue of one being the contrary of the other, such as left/right, before/after, and below/above. Bourdieu disagrees with the use of binary oppositions for the theorization of human action, as in structuralism.

Bourdieu Study Group: a study group of the British Sociological Association that brings together researchers from different disciplines to advance scholarly thought pertaining to Pierre Bourdieu.

Centre de Sociologie Européenne: a research center created by Pierre Bourdieu in 1968 to deepen the study of social reproduction. It has subsequently been united with the *Centre de Recherches Politiques de la Sorbonne.*

Collège de France: considered the most prestigious research university in France. Some on the brightest and most quoted French scholars worked and studied here.

Conscription: compulsory attendance of military service. In 1956 Bourdieu was required to serve for two years with the French Army in Algeria. It is during those years that he progressively abandoned philosophy and became interested in social science, particularly because of his life among the Kabyle.

Council estate: a neighborhood comprising houses, flats, and services provided by local municipalities and/or national governments to less resourced families. Some UK sociologists mentioned in this analysis apply Bourdieu's theory to study the reproduction of socio-economic inequality in council estates.

Cultural analysis: the analysis of data collected with qualitative methods and intended to describe and interpret the constitutive elements of human cultures. It is a form of analysis practiced in several disciplines in the humanities and social sciences, including anthropology, cultural studies, art history, comparative literature, theology, and the like.

Cultural capital: the knowledge of any kind that actors accumulate as a consequence of living in a particular context where, for example, people read newspapers, watch movies, go to the theatre, listen to music, etc. The interests of social groups are reflected in the sources of knowledge that they provide to their members who, internalizing these sources, advance the interests of their group and contribute to reproduce the overall social structure.

Determinism: the tendency to explain a phenomenon as determined by a single factor, such as environment, culture, or technology. For example, Bourdieu has been criticized for, allegedly, explaining the reproduction of socio-economic inequalities as solely determined by habitus.

Dialectic: literally, the process by which two opposing arguments are confronted in order to reach a balanced position. In the Hegelian philosophy of knowledge, the evolution of human consciousness is carried forward by means of oppositions between thesis and antithesis, resulting in a synthesis.

Dichotomy: a subdivision of a whole in two parts, implying that each of its internal components can only belong to one of the two parts. Dichotomies are a fundamental concept in structuralism because they represent the partition that the human mind operates, according to this approach, with each and every aspect of human experience, such as gender (male/female), food (raw/cooked), and kinship (marriageable/non-marriageable).

Disposition: in Bourdieu's conceptual toolkit, it indicates the tendency of actors to behave according to their habitus. Dispositions can be corporeal as well as cognitive, leading individuals to act, react, feel, and think as they do.

Doxa: in Bourdieu's terminology, the unstated, taken-for-granted assumptions of a particular group of people who are, most of the time, unable to see the arbitrariness of what they believe. Unanimous acceptance of these received ideas ensures the reproduction of socio-economic inequalities, whereas disagreement and disobedience can lead to the rearrangement of actor's positions in the class system.

École normale supérieure: one of the *Grandes Écoles* that has trained many Nobel prize laureates and prime ministers, as well as some of the most famous and quoted social scientists. Attending it was perhaps a fundamental experience for Bourdieu's career, which prepared him to become one of the most important sociologists in France and beyond.

École pratique des hautes études: one of the most prestigious research institutions in France. Bourdieu worked as Director of Studies between 1964 and 1967.

Economic capital: an accumulation of material resources, such as money and the ownership of houses, cars, businesses, and any other kind of asset that actors can dispose of as a consequence of belonging to a particular family or group. Although the reproduction of socio-economic inequality depends on the transmission of these resources from one generation to the next, Bourdieu argues that economic capital cannot by itself explain the structural and reproductive character of inequality.

Economic sociology: the discipline that explains economic phenomena as a consequence of social phenomena. With his conceptualization of different forms of capital, Bourdieu contributed to developing different directions in which the sociological study of economy can be conducted.

Elitism: the conscious or unconscious belief that a group of individual is somehow superior to another by virtue of greater material resources such a money, intellectual resources such as professional competences, or symbolic attributes such as belonging to a prestigious bloodline. Bourdieu realized how the belief in a superior class of citizen was at the origin of socio-economic inequalities when he entered the *Grandes Écoles* and, consequently, became increasingly dissatisfied with the French education system.

Empiricism: a theory of knowledge that considers direct observation as the sole method to obtain reliable knowledge. Bourdieu criticized the empiricism of ethnomethodology for lacking the ambition to turn the observed data into general theories.

Epistemology: literally, the study of how knowledge can be generated by means of scientific methods, such as direct observation, measurement, and reflection upon the perspective of the observer. With his theory of practice, Bourdieu challenged the epistemological tenets of social science and, therefore, its methods

Ethnography: literally "the written study of a people," ethnography is the text in which anthropologists present the results of their fieldwork, which is the period of qualitative research spent living among the people on which the research focuses. Bourdieu was a self-taught ethnographer because he attempted to describe the world from the point of view of the Kabyle people even though he was in Kabylia for other reasons, namely military service.

Ethnology: the comparative study of people and their culture. In France, ethnologists were particularly active in the 1950s, a time when Lévi-Strauss's structuralism was prominent theory in the discipline.

Ethnomethodology: an approach that seeks to understand human actions by means of accurate descriptions of individual practices using concepts that belong to the individual or groups under consideration, rather than the external categories of social scientists. Bourdieu also rejected the imposition of external categories, but found ethnomethodology unable to go beyond the specificities of description and generate a general theory of human action.

Existentialism: a philosophical position embodied by numerous and, in some respects, very different European thinkers of the late-nineteenth and early-twentieth centuries, which places a strong emphasis on the primacy of individual human experience. Existentialists like Jean-Paul Sartre influenced mid-twentieth century social sciences to focus on the subjectivity of individual actors, which was the approach developed by phenomenologists and ethnomethodologists.

Field: the social spaces in which actors play out their dispositions and exchange their different kinds of capital. In the original text, Bourdieu used the French term *champ* in the sense of a battlefield of competing negotiations in which actors seek to gain advantage through maneuvers that are all the more effective depending on the quantity of their social, cultural, and economic capital.

Fourth Republic: the government of France after World War II, also used to indicate the period of time between 1946 and 1958. The Fourth Republic collapsed with the political crisis that followed the Algiers coup of May 13, 1958 during the Algerian War of Independence.

Functionalism: an approach in social sciences which argues that social phenomena should be explained in terms of the function they serve to regulate and maintain society, rather than on the specific actions of individuals. Émile Durkheim is a prominent scholar in this stream.

Goffman Prize: an award given by a selected committee at the University of California, Berkeley, to researchers for their achievements in the social sciences, particularly sociology. Bourdieu received this in 1996.

Gender studies: a broad field of disciplines, such as queer studies and gay studies, that focus on people's perceptions of their own gender identity and the general representations of gender in different societies and cultures. Bourdieusian concepts, such as habitus and capital, have been used and adapted in disciplines within gender studies, such as feminist studies.

Habitus: the social actor's acquired system of lasting and transposable dispositions which, integrating past experiences, functions at every moment as a matrix of perceptions and actions. It allows social actors to unconsciously adjust between their internal subjectivity and the external objective influences, such as the family and the education system, the environment, and their peer groups.

Hegelian school: scholars who recognize themselves in the philosophy of Georg Hegel to explain the development of human consciousness as a series of successive stages, each including a thesis, an antithesis, and a synthesis. These three sub-phases express a specific moment in the development of human consciousness in the form of ideas or ideals.

Hermeneutics of suspicion: an expression used by the French philosopher Paul Ricoeur to indicate the tendency, in the writings of Karl Marx, Friedrich Nietzsche, and Sigmund Freud, to consider consciousness as illusory and a surface cover above deeper truths about human existence. Bourdieu inherited this tendency, as indicated in his conceptualization of symbolic power and doxa as mechanisms that ensure the subjugation of some members of society by means of illusory beliefs.

Historical materialism: a school of thought originated in the philosophy of Karl Marx, who saw human development through history as determined by the material relations between people and their means of production.

Huxley Medal: the highest honor awarded annually by the Royal Anthropological Institute to distinguished scholars in anthropology and related disciplines. Bourdieu received this in 2002.

Idealism: is a group of philosophies that asserts that ultimate reality as humans can perceive it, is fundamentally a mental construct, or otherwise immaterial. It is therefore dependent on the mind. It posits that ideas pre-exist matter. Hegel's idealism is an absolute version of idealism that posits the ultimate unity of thought and being.

Kabylia: a region in northern Algeria comprising part of the Tell Atlas Mountains and facing the Mediterranean Sea. During the war of independence, Kabylia was the center of the anti-colonial struggle against the French army in which Bourdieu was enlisted.

Lycée Louis-le-Grand: a prestigious secondary school comprising a sixth-form college and a post-secondary-level curriculum that prepares pupils to enter one of the *Grandes Écoles*.

Lycée: in the French education system, it is the second and last stage of secondary education, corresponding roughly to a British sixth-form college. When Bourdieu was attending the *Lycée*, though, the system was slightly different.

Management: the direction of a group of people by means of methods based on the study of human behavior in organizations. Since the beginning of the 1980s, the number of citations of Bourdieu's works in journals of managements and organization studies have been steadily growing.

Marxist: someone who identifies with the intellectual tradition inaugurated by Karl Marx, which sees society as a struggle between classes and history as a result of material relationships. Although Bourdieu inherited some conceptual tools of the Marxist tradition, he did not want to be seen as a Marxist. He thought that such qualification was only functional in making someone easier to categorize and, thus, attack.

Materialism: a philosophical approach based on the assumption that the ultimate nature of everything is physical, as opposed to idealism, which posits that ideas pre-exist matter. Karl Marx's take on Hegelian idealism is materialist to the extent that, like Hegel, Marx sees the development of human history as a sequence of rational phases, but, unlike Hegel, based on relations of production rather than an abstract thesis-antithesis-synthesis sequence.

Médaille d'or du Centre National de la Recherche Scientifique: is the highest recognition of scientific merit in France. Bourdieu was awarded it in 1993.

Objectification: the act of treating someone as an object, as opposed to an approach that attributes subjectivity and avoids the imposition of an external viewpoint, i.e. that of the objectifying observer. Bourdieu considers the objectification of social actors into social categories as ethically wrong and argues in favor of taking both the perspective of the actor and the position of the observer.

Objectivism: the conviction that it is possible to know something, or even everything, without subjective biases because reality exists independently from the human mind. Although Bourdieu intended to transcend objectivism with his theory, he has been accused of being a sophisticated objectivist.

Objectivity: the quality of a thing that is considered true regardless of subjective biases, such as individual perceptions, feelings, and emotions.

Organizational sociology: the branch of sociology that studies social behaviors in organizations, particularly the ways in which social actors interact with technological, economic, cultural, and political forces. This field has always drawn on classical studies in sociology, such as Bourdieu's *Outline*.

Patrilateral parallel cousin: in anthropological terminology, the daughter or son of one's father's brother. Bourdieu looks at the case of the marriage between patrilateral parallel cousins because it challenges some of the tenets of Lévi-Strauss's structural anthropology.

***Petit bourgeois*:** a French expression, literally meaning "small bourgeois," to indicate someone who identifies with and imitates the tastes, behaviors, and ideas of bourgeois people without actually being one of them. Bourdieu has been considered as a *petit bourgeois* even though he always declared to have a rural background.

Phenomenology: in social sciences, the study of human perception of phenomena with particular attention at the extent to which the perception can be influenced by the conditions of the observer. Bourdieu endorsed the phenomenological perspective, but only as long as it does not prevent the social scientist from theorizing phenomena as more than the mere products of subjective perceptions.

Phenomenon: in social science terminology, an event that can be perceived by the senses and can thereby be observed and studied. Bourdieu thought that all phenomena can only be observed while taking into consideration the position of the observer and the bias he inevitably introduces in the observation.

Philosophy: the study of fundamental matters, such as the nature of reason, the pursuit of knowledge, the basis of judgment, the purpose of life, and many more. Bourdieu studied philosophy but turned to anthropology in order to ground his arguments in his ethnographic experience among the Kabyles.

Positivism: the idea that it is possible to understand any aspect of the universe by means of increasingly sophisticated research methods. Objectivism, which Bourdieu rejected, is essentially an application of this idea in social sciences.

Post-modernism: a period of Western twentieth-century history characterized by a change in sensibility, practices, and discourses that marked the end of modernism in a variety of disciplines, ranging from architecture, to philosophy, literature, and art. In social sciences, post-modernism developed as a vigorous critique of abstract reason and any kind of synthetic, all-encompassing theory.

Post-positivism: in International Relations, this is the idea that positivism should be rejected. It refutes the attempt to explain international affairs and politics as if any aspects of International Relations could be understood in a complete and objective way.

Quantitative sociology: the study of human societies by means of quantitative data-collection methods, such as demographic surveys and questionnaires, which the sociologist analyzes with statistical procedures, such as linear regression.

Rational Choice Theory: also known as Rational Action Theory, this is a theory that seeks to understand how individuals take decisions concerning the best course of action for them according to a definition of rationality as a goal-oriented behavior. Bourdieu disagreed with the idea of actors as rational decision-makers and argued that they choose according to their habitus.

Relations of Production: a concept associated with Karl Marx and Friedrich Engels that refers to the social structures that regulate the relation between humans in the production of goods.

Realism: in philosophy, the belief that reality exists independently from our perception, rather than as a product of it. Bourdieu is a realist because he incorporates a certain degree of objectivism into his theory, thereby implying that reality can be known to some extent.

Social capital: the set of relationships that a single actor has with other actors and upon which they can draw in order to advance and/ or protect their interests. Bourdieu specifies that social capital can be less visible than economic capital, but not less powerful in determining the ability of actors to compete in the social field.

Social psychology: the study of the relationship between individual psychology and the social contexts in which social actors operate. While the cognitive basis of habitus remains mostly unexplored, Bourdieu's theory has been used to understand how actors internalize social patterns and externalize their own subjectivity.

Social sciences: although the term originally referred to sociology, it currently indicates many academic disciplines focused on the behavior of humans in their societies, such as anthropology, economics, psychology, political science, and even archeology, demography, and linguistics. Bourdieu has been influential well beyond the social sciences that he initially addressed with his theories, namely sociology and anthropology.

Sociology: the study of human behavior in social situations, organizations, and institutions. Although Bourdieu studied philosophy, he later became a sociologist as a consequence of the strong impact of his theories on the sociological scholarship of the time.

Structural anthropology: an anthropological approach to the study of the deepest structures of human nature below the surface of cultural phenomena.

Structuralism: a theoretical approach inspired by the structural linguistic of Ferdinand de Saussure, who distinguished between the everyday acts of speech and the underlying structure of grammar. It posits the existence of underlying structures regulating human actions, which Bourdieu regards as abstract as opposed to the concrete human actions that inform his theory of practice.

Structuration: a social theory, which gives priority neither to structure nor to agency. This approach is known to have been introduced and developed by Anthony Giddens.

Structure: Following Lévi-Strauss's formulation, the word "structure" indicates the form taken by the invariable human tendency to classify and order experience, which, conversely, is inherently variable. This formulation has been widely applied in the study of symbolism, myth, and kinship. Bourdieu noted that although structures might be an underlying set of rules that govern human actions, humans do not necessarily follow them.

Subjectivism: the tendency to explain reality in terms of a product of individual perceptions and personal experience, as opposed to objective facts that can be experienced in similar or identical ways by more than one person. Bourdieu rejected the subjectivist tendencies in phenomenological and ethnomethodological explanations of human action.

Subjectivity: the quality of an individual who is able to perceive himself or herself as a subject with a singular consciousness and the ability to express as opinion. It is a very important concept in Bourdieu's theory, for it is on subjectivity that agency is based.

Symbolic capital: the prestige and social status resulting from recognition by related actors of an individual's cultural and social capital, which Bourdieu conceptualized in order to demonstrate that power does not necessarily result from economic capital only. Although distinguished from economic capital, symbolic capital can be converted into it.

Tautology: a kind of reasoning that, albeit logical, does not explain anything and is rather circular. For example, trying to explain religion by saying that it is about religious behavior does not explain much and just re-states that which the reasoning should be intended to explain.

Third way: a perspective that transcends the normal dichotomies that one can see in traditional approaches. In *Outline* Bourdieu rejected both the way of objectivism and the way of subjectivism, and came up with a third way: the theory of practice.

PEOPLE MENTIONED IN THE TEXT

Louis Pierre Althusser (1918–90) was a French Marxist philosopher. He is best known for his structural approach to Marxism.

Aristotle (384–322 B.C.E.) was an ancient Greek philosopher who studied at Plato's academy and wrote about a wide range of topics, including physics, logic, ethics, aesthetics, and politics. Bourdieu conceptualizes habitus as a set of dispositions, which is very similar to Aristotle's concept of *hexis* as a relatively stable trait in a person's character.

Luc Boltanski (b. 1940) is a French sociologist currently professor at the *École des hautes etudes en sciences sociales*. His work has significantly influenced the fields of sociology and political economy.

Ernst Cassirer (1874–1945) was a German philosopher. He is best known for his idealist philosophy and work on the phenomenology of knowledge.

Jacques Derrida (1930–2004) was a French philosopher and one of the eminent post-modernist thinkers of the twentieth century. He is well known for his deconstructionist approach.

Émile Durkheim (1858–1917) was a French thinker who has been described as the father of sociology. He published influential works on many topics analyzing the role of social institutions in society.

Neil Fligstein (b. 1951) is an American professor of economic and political sociology at the University of California, Berkeley. In his book *The Architecture of Markets* he theorized the idea of organizational fields starting from Bourdieu's concept of field.

Michel Foucault (1926–84) was a French philosopher and social theorist whose theory mainly revolved around the role of power in societies. He studied the use of power in schools, prisons, hospitals, and other social organizations.

Georg W. F. Hegel (1770–1831) was a German philosopher. He was extremely influential with his book *Phenomenology of the Spirit*, and inspired great thinkers, such as Karl Marx.

Martin Heidegger (1889–1976) was a German philosopher. He is best known for his book *Being and Time* and for his work on hermeneutics.

Edmund Gustav Albrecht Husserl (1859–1936) was the principal founder of phenomenology and one of the most important philosophers of the twentieth century. He was very influential on the development of Martin Heidegger's existentialism.

Roman Jakobson (1896–1982) was a Russian-American linguist and literary theorist. He is best known for his structural analysis of language which was very influential on linguistics and other disciplines.

Richard Jenkins (b. 1952) is Emeritus Professor of Sociology at The University of Sheffield. In addition to his work on Bourdieu, he wrote about the transition to adulthood, the social lives of people with learning difficulties, ethnicity and racism.

Anthony King (b. 1967) was a professor in sociology at Exeter university until 2016; he currently holds a chair of war studies at Warwick University. His research focuses on sport, the transformation of armed forces, and social theory.

Michèle Lamont (b. 1957) is a Canadian professor of sociology and African American studies at Harvard University. In her book *Money, Morals and Manners*, she builds on Bourdieu's idea that shared cultural symbols reproduce class hierarchies.

Omar Lizardo (b. 1974) is Professor of Sociology at the University of Notre Dame. His research interests range from sociological theory to the sociology of culture to the philosophy of social science. He is best known for his work on the intersection between sociology and cognitive sciences.

Karl Marx (1818–83) was a German economist and social theorist. He is considered one of the most important thinkers of all time for his analysis of history as the struggle between classes, illustrated in *The Communist Manifesto* (1848).

Maurice Marleau-Ponty (1908–61) was a Marxist-influenced French phenomenological philosopher and writer who incorporated descriptive psychology into his work.

Marcel Mauss (1872–1950) is an eminent scholar in sociology and anthropology. His work *The Gift* was extremely influential and both inspired Lévi-Strauss and Bourdieu.

Jean-Claude Passeron (b. 1930) is Director of Studies at the *École des hautes etudes en sciences sociales*. He is best known for the studies he co-authored with Pierre Bourdieu.

Jean Piaget (1896–1980) was a French developmental psychologist. He is considered one of the most important scholars of the cognitive processes involved in the construction of knowledge.

Jean-Paul Sartre (1905–80) was a French philosopher and novelist well known for his contribution to existentialism, one of the dominant schools of thought in the twentieth century. He argued that human action should be understood as fundamentally free, as opposed to approaches that see it as constrained by objective limits.

Ferdinand de Saussure (1857–1913): was a Swiss linguist who conceptualized language as made of the underlying structure of grammar and the everyday act of speech. This distinction between structure and act inspired Claude Lévi-Strauss's structuralism.

Claude Lévi-Strauss (1908–2009) was a French anthropologist who devoted his life to the study of structures. He became a central figure in the structuralist school, and the most important structuralist anthropologist.

Max Weber (1864–1920) was a German scholar with interests in philosophy, economics, religion, and sociology. He is best known for his book *The Protestant Ethic and the Spirit of Capitalism.*

Loïc Wacquant (b. 1960) is professor of sociology at University of California, Berkeley. He was a student of Bourdieu and later they collaborated in some co-authored researches and publications.

WORKS CITED

WORKS CITED

Abrahams, Jessie, Nicola Ingram, Jenny Thatcher, and Ciaran Burke. *Bourdieu: The Next Generation: The Development of Bourdieu's Intellectual Heritage in Contemporary UK Sociology*. London: Routledge, 2016.

Acciaioli, Gregory L. "Knowing what you're doing: A Review of Pierre Bourdieu's Outline of a Theory of Practice." *Canberra Anthropology* 4.1 (1981): 23–51.

Adkins, Lisa, and Beverley Skeggs. eds. *Feminism after Bourdieu*. Oxford: Blackwell, 2004.

Adler-Nissen, Rebecca, ed. *Bourdieu in International Relations: Rethinking key concepts in IR*. London: Routledge, 2012.

Bourdieu, Pierre. "Célibat et condition paysanne." Études rurales. 5/6 (1962): 32–135.

— "System of Education and System of Thought." *International Social Science Journal*. XIX.3 (1967): 338–58.

— *Outline of a Theory of Practice*. Cambridge: Cambridge University Press, 1977.

— *Distinction: A Social Critique of the Judgment of Taste.* Harvard: Harvard University Press, 1984.

— "The struggle for symbolic order." *Theory, Culture and Society.* 3.3 (1986): 35–51.

— *In Other Words: Essays Toward a Reflexive Sociology.* Stanford: Stanford University Press, 1990.

— *The Logic of Practice*. Stanford: Stanford University Press, 1992.

— *Science of Science and Reflexivity*. Cambridge, Polity Press, 2004.

Bourdieu, Pierre, Jean-Claude Chamboredon, and Jean-Claude Passeron, *The Craft of Sociology: Epistemological Preliminaries.* Berlin: de Gruyter, 1991.

Bourdieu, Pierre, and Jean Claude Passeron. *The Inheritors: French Students and Their Relation to Culture.* Chicago: University of Chicago Press, 1979.

— *Reproduction in education, society and culture*. Thousand Oaks, CA: Sage, 1990.

Bourdieu, Pierre, and Loïc J.D. Wacquant. eds. *An Invitation to Reflexive Sociology*. Cambridge: Polity Press, 1992.

Bradley, Harriet, and Nicola Ingram. "Banking on the future: Choices, aspirations and economic hardship in working-class student experience." In *Class inequality in austerity Britain*, edited by Will Atkinson, Steven Roberts, and Michael Savage. London: Palgrave Macmillan, 2013: 51–69.

Calhoun, Craig. "A Different Poststructuralism." *Contemporary Sociology* 25.3 (1996): 302–305.

DiMaggio, Paul. "Cultural capital and school success: The impact of status culture participation on the grades of US high school students." *American Sociological Review* 47.2 (1982): 189–201.

Eyal, Gil, Iván Szelényi, and Eleanor R. Townsley. *Making capitalism without capitalists: Class formation and elite struggles in post-communist Central Europe*. London: Verso, 1998.

Fournier, Marcel. "Reflections on the Legacy of Pierre Bourdieu." *The Canadian Journal of Sociology/Cahiers canadiens de sociologie* 27.4 (2002): 577–581.

Garrett, Paul M. "The Relevance of Bourdieu for Social Work: A Reflection on Obstacles and Omissions." *Journal of Social Work* 7.3 (2007): 355–379.

Giddens, Anthony. *The constitution of society: Outline of a theory of structuration*. Cambridge: Polity Press, 1984.

Grenfell, Michael, and David James. *Bourdieu and Education: Acts of Practical Theory*. London: Routledge Falmer, 1998.

Grenfell, Michael. "Working with habitus and field: the logic of Bourdieu's practice." In *Cultural Analysis and Bourdieu's Legacy: Settling Accounts and Developing Alternatives*, edited by Elizabeth Silva and Alan Warde. London: Routledge, 2010: 14–27.

— *Pierre Bourdieu: Agent Provocateur.* London: Continuum, 2004.

— *Pierre Bourdieu: Key Concepts.* Durham: Acumen, 2008.

Husserl, Edmund. *Experience and Judgement*. London: Routledge and Kegan Paul, 1973.

Ingram, Nicola. "Working-class boys, educational success and the misrecognition of working-class culture." *British Journal of Sociology of Education* 30.4 (2009): 421–434.

Jenkins, Richard. *Pierre Bourdieu*. London: Routledge, 2014.

King, Anthony. "Thinking with Bourdieu against Bourdieu: A 'practical' critique of the habitus" *Sociological Theory* 18.3 (2000): 417–433.

Lamont, Michèle. "How has Bourdieu been good to think with? The case of the United States." *Sociological Forum* 27.1 (2012): 228–237.

Lave, Jean, and Etienne Wenger. *Situated learning: Legitimate peripheral participation*. Cambridge: Cambridge University Press, 1991.

Lescourret, Marie-Anne. *Bourdieu*. Paris: Flammarion, 2008.

Lizardo, Omar. "The cognitive origins of Bourdieu's habitus." *Journal for the Theory of Social Behaviour* 34.4 (2004): 375–401.

Maton, Karl. "Habitus," in *Pierre Bourdieu: Key Concepts,* edited by Michael Grenfell. Durham: Acumen, 2008: 49–65.

Nash, Roy. "Bourdieu, 'habitus', and educational research: Is it all worth the candle?" *British Journal of Sociology of Education* 20.2 (1999): 175–187.

Nice, Richard. Translator's Foreword to *Outline of a Theory of Practice* by Pierre Bourdieu, vii–viii. Cambridge: Cambridge University Press, 1977.

Rastogi, P.N. "The course of French society (1955–73) – a simulation." *Simulation* 22 (1974): 119–123.

Reay Diane, Miriam E. David, and Stephen J. Ball. *Degrees of choice: Class, race, gender and higher education*. Sterling, US: Trentham Books, 2005.

Sallaz, Jeffrey J., and Jane Zavisca. "Bourdieu in American Sociology, 1980–2004." *Annual review of sociology* 33.1 (2007): 21–41.

Schryer Catherine F., and Philippa Spoel. "Genre theory, health-care discourse, and professional identity formation." *Journal of Business and Technical Communication* 19.3 (2005): 249–278.

Silva, Elizabeth, and Alan Warde. "Introduction: the importance of Bourdieu." In *Cultural analysis and Bourdieu's legacy: settling accounts and developing alternatives*, edited by Elizabeth Silva and Alan Warde, 1–13. London: Routledge, 2010.

Sulkunen, Pekka. "Society made visible – on the cultural sociology of Pierre Bourdieu." *Acta Sociologica* 25.2 (1982): 103–115.

Susen, Simon, and Bryan S. Turner, eds. *The Legacy of Pierre Bourdieu: Critical Essays*. London: Anthem Press, 2011.

Swartz, David. "Pierre Bourdieu's Political Sociology and Public Sociology." In *Cultural analysis and Bourdieu's legacy: settling accounts and developing alternatives*, edited by Elizabeth Silva and Alan Warde, 45–59. London: Routledge, 2010.

Truong, Nicolas, and Nicolas Weill, "A decade after his death, French sociologist Pierre Bourdieu stands tall." *Guardian* 2012. Accessed July 19, 2017. https://www.theguardian.com/world/2012/feb/21/pierre-bourdieu-philosophy-most-quoted

THE MACAT LIBRARY
BY DISCIPLINE

AFRICANA STUDIES

Chinua Achebe's *An Image of Africa: Racism in Conrad's Heart of Darkness*
W. E. B. Du Bois's *The Souls of Black Folk*
Zora Neale Huston's *Characteristics of Negro Expression*
Martin Luther King Jr's *Why We Can't Wait*
Toni Morrison's *Playing in the Dark: Whiteness in the American Literary Imagination*

ANTHROPOLOGY

Arjun Appadurai's *Modernity at Large: Cultural Dimensions of Globalisation*
Philippe Ariès's *Centuries of Childhood*
Franz Boas's *Race, Language and Culture*
Kim Chan & Renée Mauborgne's *Blue Ocean Strategy*
Jared Diamond's *Guns, Germs & Steel: the Fate of Human Societies*
Jared Diamond's *Collapse: How Societies Choose to Fail or Survive*
E. E. Evans-Pritchard's *Witchcraft, Oracles and Magic Among the Azande*
James Ferguson's *The Anti-Politics Machine*
Clifford Geertz's *The Interpretation of Cultures*
David Graeber's *Debt: the First 5000 Years*
Karen Ho's *Liquidated: An Ethnography of Wall Street*
Geert Hofstede's *Culture's Consequences: Comparing Values, Behaviors, Institutes and Organizations across Nations*
Claude Lévi-Strauss's *Structural Anthropology*
Jay Macleod's *Ain't No Makin' It: Aspirations and Attainment in a Low-Income Neighborhood*
Saba Mahmood's *The Politics of Piety: The Islamic Revival and the Feminist Subjec*t
Marcel Mauss's *The Gift*

BUSINESS

Jean Lave & Etienne Wenger's *Situated Learning*
Theodore Levitt's *Marketing Myopia*
Burton G. Malkiel's *A Random Walk Down Wall Street*
Douglas McGregor's *The Human Side of Enterprise*
Michael Porter's *Competitive Strategy: Creating and Sustaining Superior Performance*
John Kotter's *Leading Change*
C. K. Prahalad & Gary Hamel's *The Core Competence of the Corporation*

CRIMINOLOGY

Michelle Alexander's *The New Jim Crow: Mass Incarceration in the Age of Colorblindness*
Michael R. Gottfredson & Travis Hirschi's *A General Theory of Crime*
Richard Herrnstein & Charles A. Murray's *The Bell Curve: Intelligence and Class Structure in American Life*
Elizabeth Loftus's *Eyewitness Testimony*
Jay Macleod's *Ain't No Makin' It: Aspirations and Attainment in a Low-Income Neighborhood*
Philip Zimbardo's *The Lucifer Effect*

ECONOMICS

Janet Abu-Lughod's *Before European Hegemony*
Ha-Joon Chang's *Kicking Away the Ladder*
David Brion Davis's *The Problem of Slavery in the Age of Revolution*
Milton Friedman's *The Role of Monetary Policy*
Milton Friedman's *Capitalism and Freedom*
David Graeber's *Debt: the First 5000 Years*
Friedrich Hayek's *The Road to Serfdom*
Karen Ho's *Liquidated: An Ethnography of Wall Street*

The Macat Library By Discipline

John Maynard Keynes's *The General Theory of Employment, Interest and Money*
Charles P. Kindleberger's *Manias, Panics and Crashes*
Robert Lucas's *Why Doesn't Capital Flow from Rich to Poor Countries?*
Burton G. Malkiel's *A Random Walk Down Wall Street*
Thomas Robert Malthus's *An Essay on the Principle of Population*
Karl Marx's *Capital*
Thomas Piketty's *Capital in the Twenty-First Century*
Amartya Sen's *Development as Freedom*
Adam Smith's *The Wealth of Nations*
Nassim Nicholas Taleb's *The Black Swan: The Impact of the Highly Improbable*
Amos Tversky's & Daniel Kahneman's *Judgment under Uncertainty: Heuristics and Biases*
Mahbub Ul Haq's *Reflections on Human Development*
Max Weber's *The Protestant Ethic and the Spirit of Capitalism*

FEMINISM AND GENDER STUDIES

Judith Butler's *Gender Trouble*
Simone De Beauvoir's *The Second Sex*
Michel Foucault's *History of Sexuality*
Betty Friedan's *The Feminine Mystique*
Saba Mahmood's *The Politics of Piety: The Islamic Revival and the Feminist Subject*
Joan Wallach Scott's *Gender and the Politics of History*
Mary Wollstonecraft's *A Vindication of the Rights of Woman*
Virginia Woolf's *A Room of One's Own*

GEOGRAPHY

The Brundtland Report's *Our Common Future*
Rachel Carson's *Silent Spring*
Charles Darwin's *On the Origin of Species*
James Ferguson's *The Anti-Politics Machine*
Jane Jacobs's *The Death and Life of Great American Cities*
James Lovelock's *Gaia: A New Look at Life on Earth*
Amartya Sen's *Development as Freedom*
Mathis Wackernagel & William Rees's *Our Ecological Footprint*

HISTORY

Janet Abu-Lughod's *Before European Hegemony*
Benedict Anderson's *Imagined Communities*
Bernard Bailyn's *The Ideological Origins of the American Revolution*
Hanna Batatu's *The Old Social Classes And The Revolutionary Movements Of Iraq*
Christopher Browning's *Ordinary Men: Reserve Police Batallion 101 and the Final Solution in Poland*
Edmund Burke's *Reflections on the Revolution in France*
William Cronon's *Nature's Metropolis: Chicago And The Great West*
Alfred W. Crosby's *The Columbian Exchange*
Hamid Dabashi's *Iran: A People Interrupted*
David Brion Davis's *The Problem of Slavery in the Age of Revolution*
Nathalie Zemon Davis's *The Return of Martin Guerre*
Jared Diamond's *Guns, Germs & Steel: the Fate of Human Societies*
Frank Dikotter's *Mao's Great Famine*
John W Dower's *War Without Mercy: Race And Power In The Pacific War*
W. E. B. Du Bois's *The Souls of Black Folk*
Richard J. Evans's *In Defence of History*
Lucien Febvre's *The Problem of Unbelief in the 16th Century*
Sheila Fitzpatrick's *Everyday Stalinism*

Eric Foner's *Reconstruction: America's Unfinished Revolution, 1863-1877*
Michel Foucault's *Discipline and Punish*
Michel Foucault's *History of Sexuality*
Francis Fukuyama's *The End of History and the Last Man*
John Lewis Gaddis's *We Now Know: Rethinking Cold War History*
Ernest Gellner's *Nations and Nationalism*
Eugene Genovese's *Roll, Jordan, Roll: The World the Slaves Made*
Carlo Ginzburg's *The Night Battles*
Daniel Goldhagen's *Hitler's Willing Executioners*
Jack Goldstone's *Revolution and Rebellion in the Early Modern World*
Antonio Gramsci's *The Prison Notebooks*
Alexander Hamilton, John Jay & James Madison's *The Federalist Papers*
Christopher Hill's *The World Turned Upside Down*
Carole Hillenbrand's *The Crusades: Islamic Perspectives*
Thomas Hobbes's *Leviathan*
Eric Hobsbawm's *The Age Of Revolution*
John A. Hobson's *Imperialism: A Study*
Albert Hourani's *History of the Arab Peoples*
Samuel P. Huntington's *The Clash of Civilizations and the Remaking of World Order*
C. L. R. James's *The Black Jacobins*
Tony Judt's *Postwar: A History of Europe Since 1945*
Ernst Kantorowicz's *The King's Two Bodies: A Study in Medieval Political Theology*
Paul Kennedy's *The Rise and Fall of the Great Powers*
Ian Kershaw's *The "Hitler Myth": Image and Reality in the Third Reich*
John Maynard Keynes's *The General Theory of Employment, Interest and Money*
Charles P. Kindleberger's *Manias, Panics and Crashes*
Martin Luther King Jr's *Why We Can't Wait*
Henry Kissinger's *World Order: Reflections on the Character of Nations and the Course of History*
Thomas Kuhn's *The Structure of Scientific Revolutions*
Georges Lefebvre's *The Coming of the French Revolution*
John Locke's *Two Treatises of Government*
Niccolò Machiavelli's *The Prince*
Thomas Robert Malthus's *An Essay on the Principle of Population*
Mahmood Mamdani's *Citizen and Subject: Contemporary Africa And The Legacy Of Late Colonialism*
Karl Marx's *Capital*
Stanley Milgram's *Obedience to Authority*
John Stuart Mill's *On Liberty*
Thomas Paine's *Common Sense*
Thomas Paine's *Rights of Man*
Geoffrey Parker's *Global Crisis: War, Climate Change and Catastrophe in the Seventeenth Century*
Jonathan Riley-Smith's *The First Crusade and the Idea of Crusading*
Jean-Jacques Rousseau's *The Social Contract*
Joan Wallach Scott's *Gender and the Politics of History*
Theda Skocpol's *States and Social Revolutions*
Adam Smith's *The Wealth of Nations*
Timothy Snyder's *Bloodlands: Europe Between Hitler and Stalin*
Sun Tzu's *The Art of War*
Keith Thomas's *Religion and the Decline of Magic*
Thucydides's *The History of the Peloponnesian War*
Frederick Jackson Turner's *The Significance of the Frontier in American History*
Odd Arne Westad's *The Global Cold War: Third World Interventions And The Making Of Our Times*

LITERATURE

Chinua Achebe's *An Image of Africa: Racism in Conrad's Heart of Darkness*
Roland Barthes's *Mythologies*
Homi K. Bhabha's *The Location of Culture*
Judith Butler's *Gender Trouble*
Simone De Beauvoir's *The Second Sex*
Ferdinand De Saussure's *Course in General Linguistics*
T. S. Eliot's *The Sacred Wood: Essays on Poetry and Criticism*
Zora Neale Huston's *Characteristics of Negro Expression*
Toni Morrison's *Playing in the Dark: Whiteness in the American Literary Imagination*
Edward Said's *Orientalism*
Gayatri Chakravorty Spivak's *Can the Subaltern Speak?*
Mary Wollstonecraft's *A Vindication of the Rights of Women*
Virginia Woolf's *A Room of One's Own*

PHILOSOPHY

Elizabeth Anscombe's *Modern Moral Philosophy*
Hannah Arendt's *The Human Condition*
Aristotle's *Metaphysics*
Aristotle's *Nicomachean Ethics*
Edmund Gettier's *Is Justified True Belief Knowledge?*
Georg Wilhelm Friedrich Hegel's *Phenomenology of Spirit*
David Hume's *Dialogues Concerning Natural Religion*
David Hume's *The Enquiry for Human Understanding*
Immanuel Kant's *Religion within the Boundaries of Mere Reason*
Immanuel Kant's *Critique of Pure Reason*
Søren Kierkegaard's *The Sickness Unto Death*
Søren Kierkegaard's *Fear and Trembling*
C. S. Lewis's *The Abolition of Man*
Alasdair MacIntyre's *After Virtue*
Marcus Aurelius's *Meditations*
Friedrich Nietzsche's *On the Genealogy of Morality*
Friedrich Nietzsche's *Beyond Good and Evil*
Plato's *Republic*
Plato's *Symposium*
Jean-Jacques Rousseau's *The Social Contract*
Gilbert Ryle's *The Concept of Mind*
Baruch Spinoza's *Ethics*
Sun Tzu's *The Art of War*
Ludwig Wittgenstein's *Philosophical Investigations*

POLITICS

Benedict Anderson's *Imagined Communities*
Aristotle's *Politics*
Bernard Bailyn's *The Ideological Origins of the American Revolution*
Edmund Burke's *Reflections on the Revolution in France*
John C. Calhoun's *A Disquisition on Government*
Ha-Joon Chang's *Kicking Away the Ladder*
Hamid Dabashi's *Iran: A People Interrupted*
Hamid Dabashi's *Theology of Discontent: The Ideological Foundation of the Islamic Revolution in Iran*
Robert Dahl's *Democracy and its Critics*
Robert Dahl's *Who Governs?*
David Brion Davis's *The Problem of Slavery in the Age of Revolution*

Alexis De Tocqueville's *Democracy in America*
James Ferguson's *The Anti-Politics Machine*
Frank Dikotter's *Mao's Great Famine*
Sheila Fitzpatrick's *Everyday Stalinism*
Eric Foner's *Reconstruction: America's Unfinished Revolution, 1863-1877*
Milton Friedman's *Capitalism and Freedom*
Francis Fukuyama's *The End of History and the Last Man*
John Lewis Gaddis's *We Now Know: Rethinking Cold War History*
Ernest Gellner's *Nations and Nationalism*
David Graeber's *Debt: the First 5000 Years*
Antonio Gramsci's *The Prison Notebooks*
Alexander Hamilton, John Jay & James Madison's *The Federalist Papers*
Friedrich Hayek's *The Road to Serfdom*
Christopher Hill's *The World Turned Upside Down*
Thomas Hobbes's *Leviathan*
John A. Hobson's *Imperialism: A Study*
Samuel P. Huntington's *The Clash of Civilizations and the Remaking of World Order*
Tony Judt's *Postwar: A History of Europe Since 1945*
David C. Kang's *China Rising: Peace, Power and Order in East Asia*
Paul Kennedy's *The Rise and Fall of Great Powers*
Robert Keohane's *After Hegemony*
Martin Luther King Jr.'s *Why We Can't Wait*
Henry Kissinger's *World Order: Reflections on the Character of Nations and the Course of History*
John Locke's *Two Treatises of Government*
Niccolò Machiavelli's *The Prince*
Thomas Robert Malthus's *An Essay on the Principle of Population*
Mahmood Mamdani's *Citizen and Subject: Contemporary Africa And The Legacy Of Late Colonialism*
Karl Marx's *Capital*
John Stuart Mill's *On Liberty*
John Stuart Mill's *Utilitarianism*
Hans Morgenthau's *Politics Among Nations*
Thomas Paine's *Common Sense*
Thomas Paine's *Rights of Man*
Thomas Piketty's *Capital in the Twenty-First Century*
Robert D. Putman's *Bowling Alone*
John Rawls's *Theory of Justice*
Jean-Jacques Rousseau's *The Social Contract*
Theda Skocpol's *States and Social Revolutions*
Adam Smith's *The Wealth of Nations*
Sun Tzu's *The Art of War*
Henry David Thoreau's *Civil Disobedience*
Thucydides's *The History of the Peloponnesian War*
Kenneth Waltz's *Theory of International Politics*
Max Weber's *Politics as a Vocation*
Odd Arne Westad's *The Global Cold War: Third World Interventions And The Making Of Our Times*

POSTCOLONIAL STUDIES

Roland Barthes's *Mythologies*
Frantz Fanon's *Black Skin, White Masks*
Homi K. Bhabha's *The Location of Culture*
Gustavo Gutiérrez's *A Theology of Liberation*
Edward Said's *Orientalism*
Gayatri Chakravorty Spivak's *Can the Subaltern Speak?*

The Macat Library By Discipline

PSYCHOLOGY

Gordon Allport's *The Nature of Prejudice*
Alan Baddeley & Graham Hitch's *Aggression: A Social Learning Analysis*
Albert Bandura's *Aggression: A Social Learning Analysis*
Leon Festinger's *A Theory of Cognitive Dissonance*
Sigmund Freud's *The Interpretation of Dreams*
Betty Friedan's *The Feminine Mystique*
Michael R. Gottfredson & Travis Hirschi's *A General Theory of Crime*
Eric Hoffer's *The True Believer: Thoughts on the Nature of Mass Movements*
William James's *Principles of Psychology*
Elizabeth Loftus's *Eyewitness Testimony*
A. H. Maslow's *A Theory of Human Motivation*
Stanley Milgram's *Obedience to Authority*
Steven Pinker's *The Better Angels of Our Nature*
Oliver Sacks's *The Man Who Mistook His Wife For a Hat*
Richard Thaler & Cass Sunstein's *Nudge: Improving Decisions About Health, Wealth and Happiness*
Amos Tversky's *Judgment under Uncertainty: Heuristics and Biases*
Philip Zimbardo's *The Lucifer Effect*

SCIENCE

Rachel Carson's *Silent Spring*
William Cronon's *Nature's Metropolis: Chicago And The Great West*
Alfred W. Crosby's *The Columbian Exchange*
Charles Darwin's *On the Origin of Species*
Richard Dawkin's *The Selfish Gene*
Thomas Kuhn's *The Structure of Scientific Revolutions*
Geoffrey Parker's *Global Crisis: War, Climate Change and Catastrophe in the Seventeenth Century*
Mathis Wackernagel & William Rees's *Our Ecological Footprint*

SOCIOLOGY

Michelle Alexander's *The New Jim Crow: Mass Incarceration in the Age of Colorblindness*
Gordon Allport's *The Nature of Prejudice*
Albert Bandura's *Aggression: A Social Learning Analysis*
Hanna Batatu's *The Old Social Classes And The Revolutionary Movements Of Iraq*
Ha-Joon Chang's *Kicking Away the Ladder*
W. E. B. Du Bois's *The Souls of Black Folk*
Émile Durkheim's *On Suicide*
Frantz Fanon's *Black Skin, White Masks*
Frantz Fanon's *The Wretched of the Earth*
Eric Foner's *Reconstruction: America's Unfinished Revolution, 1863-1877*
Eugene Genovese's *Roll, Jordan, Roll: The World the Slaves Made*
Jack Goldstone's *Revolution and Rebellion in the Early Modern World*
Antonio Gramsci's *The Prison Notebooks*
Richard Herrnstein & Charles A Murray's *The Bell Curve: Intelligence and Class Structure in American Life*
Eric Hoffer's *The True Believer: Thoughts on the Nature of Mass Movements*
Jane Jacobs's *The Death and Life of Great American Cities*
Robert Lucas's *Why Doesn't Capital Flow from Rich to Poor Countries?*
Jay Macleod's *Ain't No Makin' It: Aspirations and Attainment in a Low Income Neighborhood*
Elaine May's *Homeward Bound: American Families in the Cold War Era*
Douglas McGregor's *The Human Side of Enterprise*
C. Wright Mills's *The Sociological Imagination*

Thomas Piketty's *Capital in the Twenty-First Century*
Robert D. Putman's *Bowling Alone*
David Riesman's *The Lonely Crowd: A Study of the Changing American Character*
Edward Said's *Orientalism*
Joan Wallach Scott's *Gender and the Politics of History*
Theda Skocpol's *States and Social Revolutions*
Max Weber's *The Protestant Ethic and the Spirit of Capitalism*

THEOLOGY

Augustine's *Confessions*
Benedict's *Rule of St Benedict*
Gustavo Gutiérrez's *A Theology of Liberation*
Carole Hillenbrand's *The Crusades: Islamic Perspectives*
David Hume's *Dialogues Concerning Natural Religion*
Immanuel Kant's *Religion within the Boundaries of Mere Reason*
Ernst Kantorowicz's *The King's Two Bodies: A Study in Medieval Political Theology*
Søren Kierkegaard's *The Sickness Unto Death*
C. S. Lewis's *The Abolition of Man*
Saba Mahmood's *The Politics of Piety: The Islamic Revival and the Feminist Subjec*t
Baruch Spinoza's *Ethics*
Keith Thomas's *Religion and the Decline of Magic*

COMING SOON

Chris Argyris's *The Individual and the Organisation*
Seyla Benhabib's *The Rights of Others*
Walter Benjamin's *The Work Of Art in the Age of Mechanical Reproduction*
John Berger's *Ways of Seeing*
Pierre Bourdieu's *Outline of a Theory of Practice*
Mary Douglas's *Purity and Danger*
Roland Dworkin's *Taking Rights Seriously*
James G. March's *Exploration and Exploitation in Organisational Learning*
Ikujiro Nonaka's *A Dynamic Theory of Organizational Knowledge Creation*
Griselda Pollock's *Vision and Difference*
Amartya Sen's *Inequality Re-Examined*
Susan Sontag's *On Photography*
Yasser Tabbaa's *The Transformation of Islamic Art*
Ludwig von Mises's *Theory of Money and Credit*

Macat Disciplines

Access the greatest ideas and thinkers across entire disciplines, including

FEMINISM, GENDER AND QUEER STUDIES

Simone De Beauvoir's
The Second Sex

Michel Foucault's
History of Sexuality

Betty Friedan's
The Feminine Mystique

Saba Mahmood's
*The Politics of Piety:
The Islamic Revival and
the Feminist Subject*

Joan Wallach Scott's
*Gender and the
Politics of History*

Mary Wollstonecraft's
*A Vindication of the
Rights of Woman*

Virginia Woolf's
A Room of One's Own

Judith Butler's
Gender Trouble

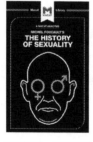

Macat analyses are available from all good bookshops and libraries.

Access hundreds of analyses through one, multimedia tool.
Join free for one month **library.macat.com**

Macat Disciplines

*Access the greatest ideas and thinkers
across entire disciplines, including*

INEQUALITY

Ha-Joon Chang's, *Kicking Away the Ladder*

David Graeber's, *Debt: The First 5000 Years*

Robert E. Lucas's, *Why Doesn't Capital Flow from
Rich To Poor Countries?*

Thomas Piketty's, *Capital in the Twenty-First Century*

Amartya Sen's, *Inequality Re-Examined*

Mahbub Ul Haq's, *Reflections on Human Development*

Macat analyses are available from all good bookshops and libraries.

Access hundreds of analyses through one, multimedia tool.
Join free for one month **library.macat.com**

Macat Disciplines

Access the greatest ideas and thinkers across entire disciplines, including

CRIMINOLOGY

Michelle Alexander's
The New Jim Crow: Mass Incarceration in the Age of Colorblindness

Michael R. Gottfredson & Travis Hirschi's
A General Theory of Crime

Elizabeth Loftus's
Eyewitness Testimony

Richard Herrnstein & Charles A. Murray's
The Bell Curve: Intelligence and Class Structure in American Life

Jay Macleod's
Ain't No Makin' It: Aspirations and Attainment in a Low-Income Neighborhood

Philip Zimbardo's
The Lucifer Effect

Macat analyses are available from all good bookshops and libraries.

Access hundreds of analyses through one, multimedia tool.
Join free for one month **library.macat.com**

Macat Disciplines

Access the greatest ideas and thinkers across entire disciplines, including

Postcolonial Studies

Roland Barthes's *Mythologies*
Frantz Fanon's *Black Skin, White Masks*
Homi K. Bhabha's *The Location of Culture*
Gustavo Gutiérrez's *A Theology of Liberation*
Edward Said's *Orientalism*
Gayatri Chakravorty Spivak's *Can the Subaltern Speak?*

Macat Disciplines

Access the greatest ideas and thinkers
across entire disciplines, including

GLOBALIZATION

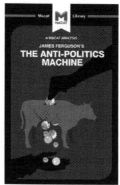

Arjun Appadurai's, *Modernity at Large:*
Cultural Dimensions of Globalisation

James Ferguson's, *The Anti-Politics Machine*

Geert Hofstede's, *Culture's Consequences*

Amartya Sen's, *Development as Freedom*

Macat analyses are available from all good bookshops and libraries.

Access hundreds of analyses through one, multimedia tool.
Join free for one month **library.macat.com**

Macat Pairs

Analyse historical and modern issues from opposite sides of an argument. Pairs include:

HOW TO RUN AN ECONOMY

John Maynard Keynes's
The General Theory OF Employment, Interest and Money

Classical economics suggests that market economies are self-correcting in times of recession or depression, and tend toward full employment and output. But English economist John Maynard Keynes disagrees.

In his ground-breaking 1936 study *The General Theory*, Keynes argues that traditional economics has misunderstood the causes of unemployment. Employment is not determined by the price of labor; it is directly linked to demand. Keynes believes market economies are by nature unstable, and so require government intervention. Spurred on by the social catastrophe of the Great Depression of the 1930s, he sets out to revolutionize the way the world thinks

Milton Friedman's
The Role of Monetary Policy

Friedman's 1968 paper changed the course of economic theory. In just 17 pages, he demolished existing theory and outlined an effective alternate monetary policy designed to secure 'high employment, stable prices and rapid growth.'

Friedman demonstrated that monetary policy plays a vital role in broader economic stability and argued that economists got their monetary policy wrong in the 1950s and 1960s by misunderstanding the relationship between inflation and unemployment. Previous generations of economists had believed that governments could permanently decrease unemployment by permitting inflation—and vice versa. Friedman's most original contribution was to show that this supposed trade-off is an illusion that only works in the short term.

Printed in the United States
by Baker & Taylor Publisher Services